CHARLES SCHWAB'S

GUIDE TO FINANCIAL

INDEPENDENCE

■ ■ ■ ■ ■

CHARLES SCHWAB'S
GUIDE TO FINANCIAL
INDEPENDENCE

■ ■ ■ ■ ■

Simple Solutions for Busy People

BY

CHARLES R. SCHWAB

CROWN PUBLISHERS, INC.
NEW YORK

Published by Crown Publishers, Inc., 201 East 50th Street, New York, New York 10022. Member of the Crown Publishing Group.

Random House, Inc. New York, Toronto, London, Sydney, Auckland
www.randomhouse.com

CROWN and colophon are trademarks of Crown Publishers, Inc.

Printed in the United States of America

Designed by Robert Bull Design

Library of Congress Cataloging-in-Publication Data
Schwab, Charles.
Charles Schwab's guide to financial independence : simple solutions for busy people.
Includes index.
1. Finance, Personal. 2. Stocks. I. Title.
HG179.S334   1998
332.024—dc21   97–34870

ISBN 0-609-60124-5

10 9 8 7 6 5 4 3 2 1

First Edition

DEDICATION

I dedicate this book to my beloved wife, Helen, who has encouraged and supported me through my lifelong pursuit of investing, and to my kids and grandkids, who are my biggest dividend.

ACKNOWLEDGMENTS

As anyone who has attempted it knows, writing a book is hardly a solitary activity. In writing this book, I owe thanks and acknowledgment to four sources of great help. Bo Caldwell put my thoughts on paper and shaped and polished the prose; and Nicole Young guided the book through the process, from idea to final manuscript. My thanks also go to the employees of Charles Schwab & Co. for their dedicated customer service and their commitment to acting as the custodians of our customers' financial dreams. And lastly, my thanks go to our customers, the thousands of people who have trusted us with those dreams.

CONTENTS

PROLOGUE

Dear Reader,

You're in your prime, with a full-time job and maybe a full-time marriage and full-time kids to match, and everything's under control, right? Well, *almost* everything. There's just one area of your life that you haven't addressed as you should: investing for your future. You've done something: You probably have an IRA and a 401(k) at work. Maybe you've invested in a favorite stock and a couple of mutual funds. But there's still this nagging feeling that it's not enough, and even though you know that's true, you're not doing anything about it.

Why? Why do so many people put investing at the bottom of the list? Time, of course, is one reason; a lot of people feel that they just don't have the time to learn. But it's more than that. There's a perception that investing is only for the pros, a sort of *don't-try-this-at-home* endeavor. People are intimidated, and it's the same kind of intimidation that keeps us from trying anything we perceive as being too difficult, even when we see quite plainly that a lot of people around us are doing it well. If you're a high achiever type—

if you take pride in excelling at whatever you do—it's even worse, because investing appears to be the kind of thing that takes years to really master, and why do something at all if you can't do it well? Whether we're on the job or on the golf course, in the courtroom or the kitchen, we like to do well, and the idea of investing threatens our confidence. A lot of people would no more consider trying their hand at the stock market than they'd consider acting as their own attorney.

But here's news from the front: What intimidates people about investing is largely myth, a web of misconceptions that has been around so long and has become so pervasive as to seem unquestionable. People think the stock market's too risky, they don't speak the language, they don't know enough about economics. All common ideas, and all untrue, because the good news—the really *great* news, actually—is that investing is easily demystified. Although a lot of brokers wish it were otherwise (and work very hard and make a lot of money by convincing you that investing is magic that only *they* know), investing wisely just isn't that hard. It's like buying a car: You don't want to do it on a whim, or without some research, but it's certainly doable. You just have to do a little homework, and it doesn't demand a background in finance. You don't have to give up your regular life or quit your day job. You just have to pay attention, and the main thing you need is something you've already got: simple common sense. Add to that some guidance from this book, and you're well on your way. And once you've gotten started, investing is simply a matter of maintenance, like getting a checkup, or having the oil changed, or taking the dog to the vet. No more, no less. No magic. It's just something you have to do on a regular basis.

The key is to get started, and to do it now, because that's how you avoid the biggest risk, the risk of doing nothing, and watching inflation eat up your money. You're skeptical? Go to a senior center at lunch. You'll see senior citizens who, through bad luck or unfortunate circumstances or inadequate planning, have to come to these centers for a free hot meal. They're making do, but just barely, because the fact is that for those past 65, getting along financially is getting harder all the time. Think about your parents, or your grandparents, who maybe put aside some savings and depended on Social Security or maybe even other family members—and managed to get by. But things have changed. Americans are living longer. We're healthier—60 isn't old anymore. Think of your mother at 60 compared with your grandmother at 60. And college costs, for our kids, are beyond our parents' wildest imagination.

That's the reason for planning ahead: to avoid getting caught unprepared. The idea of aging is sobering, I admit, and it's another reason people avoid thinking about this part of their lives. Our fears about addressing the future aren't just about money. They're about change and getting older, and while we all know that those issues can be difficult to think about, facing them's a lot better than stuffing them in the closet. Things get a little easier once you've started planning. You relax a little, because you learn that this is an area of your life where you have some control. Fix what you can, right? Right, but not with a quick fix, and not for a quick buck. Investing isn't a game; it's for keeps, a long-term commitment that involves a simple reordering of financial priorities. And while you may have to give a little—to cut back on the annual getaway or the feel-good spending—you'll get a lot more. When that monthly statement comes and you see your money growing, you rest easier because you're doing things right: you're planning for your future.

If I sound passionate about this, I am. I remind my employees that we are the custodians of our customers' financial dreams, and it's not something I take lightly. When I see elderly people lining up for a free lunch at a senior center, my heart goes out to them. I've spent 40 years living and breathing investing; I know what to do, and I'm eager to pass on what I've learned. I could explain most of what you need to know over a long lunch.

Think of this book as everything I would share with you during that lunch. Read it. Try out the suggestions. But please, *do something*, because the biggest risk in investing is doing nothing. You've got to start; as soon as you do, you're two steps closer to your hopes of financial security.

Charles R Schwab

P.S. If you feel pressed for time, don't give up. Give yourself 30 minutes, and read Chapter 1. When you finish, you'll be on your way.

"A journey of a thousand miles
must begin with a single step."
—Lao-Tzu

I

INVESTING
MADE
EASY

1

IT'S ALL ABOUT GROWTH

What do you think of when you hear the word *invest?* The books-and-movies scenes showing the chaotic floor of the New York Stock Exchange? Stock certificates? The financial pages of the newspaper? Not me. When I think of investing, I think of *growth,* because to me that's at the very heart of successful investing. And strange as it may sound, I mean the kind of growth that's all around us, the growth we see every day in trees and plants and our kids.

Think of biology. Maybe you've observed under a microscope the amazing spectacle of an amoeba dividing itself into two. There it is, this tiny one-celled organism, and at some point, right before your eyes, it reproduces by dividing itself. All of a sudden where there was one amoeba, now there are two. You keep watching, and soon the two become four, and the four become eight, and the eight sixteen— and you're seeing this incredible example of growth. Here's an organism that's growing at a geometric rate—1, 2, 4, 8, 16!—dou- bling itself each time.

What does that have to do with investing? A lot. An amoeba is an organism that divides itself into something more than it was before—and that, to my mind, is exactly what a company is: an organism that grows. When you invest in stock, you're buying shares of ownership of a company, and that's where growth comes in: You now own a part of something that's alive and growing. The first year the company has five employees, maybe one product, 20 customers, and a rented building. Next year maybe it has 12 employees, three products, and 50 customers. The company helps itself to grow by reinvesting a sizable portion of its profits, fueling its future growth. It's growth on top of growth, and it's a phenomenon that holds me in awe. *Growth* is what successful investing is all about.

I'm 60 years old as I write this book, and I've been studying investing for 40 years. During that time I've had the pleasure and sometimes the sorrow of investing in a lot of different companies, and I've probably studied investing as intensely as just about anybody around. I've studied both by watching—by observing the companies around me—and by doing—by actively founding and building companies, including serving on the boards of major public companies, some of them 100 years old, some 25, some less than 2. Most of those companies have become successful, although a few haven't.

In those 40 years, I've developed an approach to investing that's simple and straightforward, centered on the notion of growth. There are, admittedly, more complex approaches out there, but why complicate things when you don't have to? The world of investing is fascinating, but it can soak up as much time as you're willing to give to it.

If you did what I've done over these years, maybe you'd come up with the same simplified approach. But 40 years is a long time to wait. So I'm hoping to save you some time; I'm hoping my experience can be of benefit to you.

WHY STOCKS?

Put simply, my belief is that of all the many investments available, stocks provide the best chance for growth over time. They are a great solution for long-term investing. This conviction lies at the very core of my approach, and while this may sound self-serving, coming from the founder of a brokerage business, my reason for saying so is very simple: I am a firm believer in the wealth-generating power of stocks, a belief that has only grown stronger with time.

The reasons for that belief are tantamount to the fundamentals of the religion. They define a position that I absolutely believe in, and it's a position that you, the reader, have to understand if you are to benefit from this book. More than understand, you have to have confidence in this approach as well, and you have to feel that confidence in your very core, because you will be tested. And if your confidence is low, you'll panic and be tempted to run at the first downturn of the market.

We start with a fact: Over time, stocks have outperformed all other kinds of investments, including bonds, CDs, and U.S. government securities. How do we know this? A little stock market history backs it up. Jeremy Siegel, a professor of finance at the Wharton School, looked at stock market returns from 1802 to 1996 and found that in total returns stocks outperformed all other types of assets. "One dollar invested and reinvested in stocks since 1802 would have accumulated to $5,610,000 by the end of 1996," he writes. The chart "Total Nominal Return Indices," taken from Siegel's book *Stocks for the Long Run,* gives a vivid picture. (See page 22.)

As you can see, the long-term trend of the stock market in the United States has always been upward. Yes, there've been ups and significant down periods, but over the long haul the trend is up, and it's a pretty good track record.

Now that simple fact alone—*over time, stocks have outperformed all other kinds of investments*—in and of itself makes a pretty good case for investing in stocks. It's historical evidence, and it's great, but how do we know the upward trend will continue? How can we be sure? Yes, we can see it on paper; we can look at that chart and see the evidence, but the question is *why?* Why have stocks outperformed other kinds of investments? Is it luck? Coincidence? Magic? Government regulations?

None of the above. There's no voodoo, no hocus pocus, no tricks, and no mirrors. It's not even much of a mystery. There's a reason for that continuous upward trend. It's what distinguishes stocks from all other investments, and it's the same reason they've proven to be such solid investments over time. And it is, to me, the best argument for investing in stocks.

It's growth.

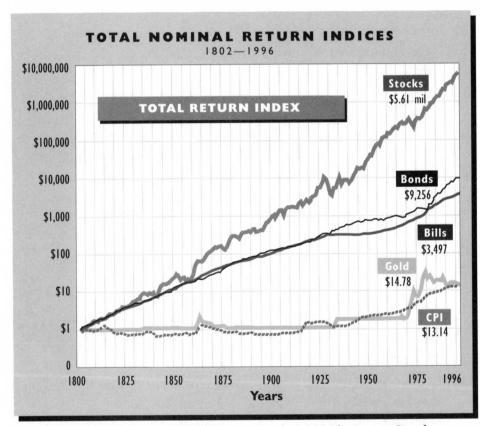

From *Stocks for the Long Run* by Jeremy Siegel, © 1994 by Jeremy Siegel. Reproduced with permission of the McGraw-Hill Companies.

MAKING SURE WE'RE ON THE SAME PAGE

At the end of this book, you'll find a Glossary that gives concise, accurate definitions of the terms most commonly used in investing. You may find it helpful to turn to it as you read the book. But first things first; sometimes even investing's household words can cause confusion because they're often used in more than one context. So at the outset I want to make sure you understand how I'm using some of the basic words:

STOCK

A fractional ownership in a company, measured by one or more shares.

STOCKS

Lots of companies in which you can invest. When I say someone owns stocks, I mean that they own shares in many companies.

COMPANY

A corporation that is formed with some business venture as its goal. In everyday parlance, a stock and a company are basically the same. "IBM" refers to both the company and the stock.

STOCK MARKET

The broadly diversified inventory of publicly owned companies. For example, the S&P 500 and the Schwab 1000 are broad representations of the greater stock market.

EARNINGS PER SHARE

A company's net income divided by the number of its common shares outstanding. For example, $1 million net income divided by 1 million shares outstanding equals $1 earnings per share.

DIVIDEND

The part of a company's net income distributed to shareholders.

BOND

An IOU issued by the federal and/or a local government or a corporation. The bond states that you have loaned money to the borrower and that you will be paid back on a certain date and at a certain rate of interest.

■ ■ ■ ■ ■ ■ ■ ■ ■ ■ ■ ■ ■ ■ ■ ■ ■ ■ ■ ■

THE GENETIC ENGINEERING OF STOCKS

Every investment book talks about the superior performance of stocks and stock mutual funds over every other kind of investment. You can see this performance when you study stock market price records for the last 10 or 50 or 100 years, and by studying those records, you'd probably reach an empirical conclusion. I'd like to take it a step further: I'm interested in the *why*. Why does growth cause stocks to consistently outperform other investments over the long term?

When you invest in a stock, you're buying part of a company. You buy a certain number of shares that represent a small portion of the total ownership of the company. A company is a wonderful creation that has been genetically formed to grow; that's what it's designed to do. It is the task of management and the board of directors to oversee and encourage and enable that growth. I've been on a number of company boards, both public and private, and during all these years, I've never heard a management team come into the boardroom and announce that the company would strive to remain static for the upcoming year, that no growth was planned. I've never heard anything less than a plan for 10% growth. Now, the company may not meet its goal or it may exceed its mark, but the point is that business is about growth.

And companies do just that: They get bigger. I think of companies as living organisms because they grow in so many ways: in number of employees, revenues, net worth, number of products produced and shipped, services offered, operating plants or factories, and—most important—the number of customers. Companies even grow physically.

When you buy stock in a company, you're buying part of that organism. Next year the company might be 10% larger than it is now, and soon it could be 25% bigger than it was two years ago. If you're a shareholder, your share of wealth will grow as the company grows. Your investment may not grow overnight (or it may); it may take two steps forward and one step back. It may even reach a plateau now and then. But over a five-to-ten-year period, the chances are that it will grow. You just have to be patient.

Companies need fuel to grow, and amazingly, they are genetically coded to fuel themselves. How? Instead of paying out all of its profits to shareholders (as dividends), a company can reinvest that money into itself—it can feed its own growth. A company that paid out 100% of its earnings in dividends couldn't sustain growth. It would have no fuel. But if it paid only 25% in dividends, then 75% of its net income would be plowed back into its own growth. *And that's fuel*—the company puts that money right back to work, so that it continues to compound, feeding the company, helping it to grow. (An equation called the ROE, which stands for "return on equity"—the net income of a company divided by its net worth—is, in my mind, the single best indicator of a company's growth potential.)

All of which makes stocks fundamentally—I say *genetically*—different from all other investment alternatives, including money market funds, bonds, CDs, government bonds, and real estate. When you put your money in a CD or a money market account in a bank, you aren't buying anything. You're simply loaning your money to someone who's willing to pay you some interest on it. (If the bank then takes your money and loans it out to other people or companies, it makes a profit off the difference.) Your interest rate is predetermined and limited, and by convention, it runs a point or two higher than inflation.

When you invest in real estate, it's true, you are buying something tangible. Say you buy an apartment building. Over time, with inflation, it might go up in value. Maybe you buy it for $100,000, and inflation goes from 3% to 5%, and the community goes slightly upscale, so in ten years the building's worth $150,000. That's great, but you know what? That apartment building hasn't grown. The square footage hasn't gotten any bigger.

But with a company, the whole idea is for it to get bigger. A company that starts out with one product in the first year might have two products the next year. It starts out with five people, then goes to 10, 15, 20. And as its revenues grow, its profits grow, and at the end of the year, management comes in to the board of directors and says, "Hey, we're planning on growing by 15% next year!" to which you say, "Let's go!" because everybody involved—the board of directors, management, the employees, shareholders like you—wants the same thing: they want that company to grow.

Let's say an average American company grows at the rate of 11% per annum. Maybe 3% of that is inflation and 8% is real growth. At 11% growth, you, the shareholder, might be paid a 2% dividend, and the company reinvests 9% back into growing the company. The reinvestment fuels the company as it expands, by building new plants and new equipment and by offering new services. Over time, you probably get an average of 9–11% *compounded* return. No other financial instrument features this same genetic engineering.

Consider another hypothetical example. Company A stock earned $1 per share after tax, and it paid a dividend of $.20 per share. It had a book value (its net worth divided by the number of shares outstanding) per share of $8. So Company A had a rate of return on capital of $1 divided by $8, which equals 12.5%—a nice return, and one that approximates the historical return on American companies.

The next year, Company A reinvests the remaining earnings from the previous year, $.80 per share, in new plant equipment and services for its expanding list of customers. This means, of course, that the company is reinvesting 80% of its net earnings for its future growth after having paid out 20% of those earnings in a cash dividend.

In the following year Company A shows another nice growth rate of at least 10%. Its earnings are $1.10 for that year. Management once again pays out 20% in dividends and reinvests the balance in future growth. The company's annual comparative growth goes on like this for the indefinite future. (This scenario assumes that the management of Company A is reasonably astute, and that a little kicker of 2.5–3% inflation is thrown in.)

One year Company A offers another type of investment: corporate bonds traded on the New York Bond Exchange. The bonds provide investors with a 7.5% return, so after paying personal taxes, investors might net 5%. Now the person interested in investing in Company A has to make a choice between an investment (in stocks) that will grow at 10–12% per annum after taxes and one (in bonds) that will pay out at 5% after taxes. Seems to me like a pretty simple choice: The corporate bond will pay its interest every year right on time, but it will never grow. From year to year, the company's stock value will change, but it will appreciate in line with the company growth rate. Its future growth parallels and is closely dependent upon the rate of return on capital being achieved each year—in this case, 12.5%. Stocks will always be more volatile from year to year than bonds, a factor that alarms a lot of people. But such variations vide the opportunity for those who understand the genetics of cks to become confident and lifelong investors. And while I've oversimplified this example of Company A, it's pretty close to what really happens. Bonds are made to pay interest, while stocks are made to grow.

Most average companies seem able to sustain a growth rate of 8% to 10%. The top 5% of corporate America has a much higher growth rate, but higher rates are difficult to sustain. My own company grows in excess of 20% per year. We give fuel a high priority. We reinvest 90% of our cash flow into new things—like technology, new products and services, and new businesses—with astute management figuring out wise places to invest that money. But there are, of course, limits to growth; the beanstalk doesn't reach to the sky. Chances are that someday management won't be so astute, and my own company won't continue to grow at such a high rate. Across the board of S&P 500 companies, astute management has, on average, been able to grow their company and get returns on capital in the 10–15% range.

THE INFLATION HEDGE

Inflation: sounds relatively harmless, but when it comes to investing, it's far from harmless. It's always there, and it always will be, like a small leak you can't fix, only it gets bigger with time, because inflation compounds every year. Even at the low rate of 3% per annum, inflation eats up more than a third of your money's purchasing power every ten years. In twenty-four years, your money will be worth only half as much as it is now. That's a pretty big number in my book, and that's inflation at a conservative 3%. Watch what happens when that number begins to climb. At 5% your purchasing power is cut in half in 14 years, and at 6% it's 12 years. And I haven't even mentioned the effect of taxes yet, the largest single drag on your investments.

Startled? A lot of people are, when they hear about inflation's corrosive effect, and with good reason. When you get a sneaking suspicion that your money just isn't going as far as it used to, well, you're right. It *isn't* going as far, simply because it has less purchasing power. (Strangely enough, governments consider some inflation to be good, and they seem to like to err on the side of a little inflation. If price levels go *down* 3% a year, it makes people feel slightly depressed. But if everything goes up a small amount each year—say, 3%, which is where the U.S. government tries to keep inflation—people seem to feel better, because even their salaries increase slightly.)

Another reason that stocks grow is that inflation is built right into the return of a stock. When it comes to investing, inflation takes its toll, but it takes a greater toll on bonds than on stocks. Good companies can adjust to inflation; they change their prices or cut their costs to compensate for it. Unlike bank-paid interest and bonds, which will often match or do a little better than inflation, companies have the ability to change their pricing and stay ahead of it. Look at Coca-Cola. The cost of a bottle of Coke was about five cents back in 1950; now that same soft drink sells for around a dollar a bottle, which means that through the years, it's been adjusted for inflation.

* * *

For all these reasons, I'm an enthusiast about stocks, whether you buy them individually or in mutual funds. What I am suggesting is a systematic and reasonable method of investing, one that's light-years from Las Vegas. It's a purposeful and well-thought-out method of investing in solid, growing companies.

And it means investing for the long term. It doesn't mean making a quick kill. It means accepting the fact that investing is not an overnight phenomenon. It's a financial commitment of at least seven years; longer is even better. Once you are committed to the long term, the ups and downs of the market won't get to you as much, because you will recognize that they're just part of the deal. If you learn to hold on through the down periods, after the first couple of business cycles, you'll gain some confidence and the fluctuations won't throw you. When you make a long-term commitment, you just wait, knowing you've made the right choice.

If you want your money to grow at a rate that gives you a nice straight line tilted at a very gentle upward slope, with no downs, just a gradual increase, put it in a savings account and leave it there. If, on the other hand, you want your money to grow, put it in something that's made to grow: stocks.

■ ■ ■ ■ ■ ■ ■ ■ ■ ■ ■ ■ ■ ■ ■ ■ ■ ■ ■ ■

SEEING THE GROWTH

The chart below shows the growth phenomenon I've been talking about. It chronicles the earnings per share (EPS) of all 500 companies in the S&P 500 Index at 5-year intervals for the last 50 years.

STANDARD & POOR'S 500 COMPOSITE
ANNUAL EARNINGS PER SHARE

1996	$38.73
1991	15.97
1986	14.48
1981	15.36
1976	9.91
1971	5.70
1966	5.55
1961	3.19
1956	3.41
1951	2.44
1946	1.06
1941	0.96
1936	1.00
1931	0.61
1926	1.24

A company's EPS is calculated by dividing its total after-tax profits by the number of common shares of its stock outstanding. A rising EPS is an indication of greater profitability for the company. An improvement in profitability from the same quarter a year earlier is often seen before a company's stock rises substantially. A stock becomes a great investment when the company's continued growth in earnings drives it to make more money for its shareholders.

The increase in EPS from year to year, as seen in the chart, is evidence that the market as a whole (as represented by the S&P 500 Index) is growing. And that's why stocks have such a huge advantage over other types of investments. Whether we're talking about an individual stock or the market in the aggregate, a steadily rising EPS is evidence of growth and profitability.

THE NATURE OF THE BEAST WE CALL THE STOCK MARKET

What exactly *is* the stock market? The way some people talk, it almost seems to have a personality at times, alternately bullish and bearish. It's certainly an entity with a history.

A QUICK HISTORY LESSON

The origin of the stock market is uncertain, but it's believed that securities were sold in the streets of Rome during the days of the Roman Empire. The first stock exchange in Europe was established at Antwerp, Belgium, in 1531, and a securities market was operating in Amsterdam as early as 1602. Trading in securities in England was conducted by "stock jobbers" as early as 1688, and in 1773 the brokers of London formed England's first stock exchange. Until then, people who wanted to buy or sell stock had to seek out a broker to make the transaction.

The stock market has been a part of American history from the start. When the Plymouth Company sent the Pilgrims to America, each of them received a share of its stock. Securities were traded in New York as early as 1725, and the first stock exchange was formed in Philadelphia in 1790. By the next year, stock quotations were being printed in American newspapers, and in 1792 a group of brokers who met under an old buttonwood tree on Wall Street executed what became known as the Buttonwood Agreement, which led to the formation of the New York Stock Exchange. (The American Stock Exchange was originally called the Curb Exchange because of its origin on the streets of New York City.) By 1800 there were more than 350 profit-making corporations in the United States, and 15 years later there were eight brokerage firms in New York. But business could be slow; on a day in 1830, for example, only 31 shares were traded.

The part of stock market history that most of us are familiar with is the crash of 1929. President Franklin D. Roosevelt's subsequent New Deal legislation was designed to prevent a recurrence of the excesses that led to the crash, and the Securities Exchange Act of 1934, part of the New Deal legislation, was passed to regulate the stock exchanges and broker-dealers. Both were required to register with the newly created Securities and Exchange Commission (SEC).

Another piece of New Deal legislation, the Securities Act of 1933, sought to add "to the ancient rule of caveat emptor (let the buyer beware) the further doctrine 'let the seller also beware.' " This act was intended to put the "burden of telling the whole truth on the seller." It required that companies register new issues of securities with the SEC before selling them to the public and offer prospectuses providing full disclosure. Recovery from the crash of 1929 was slow; some people feel haunted by the Great Depression even today. Still, the fact is that the market not only recovered but, over time, has thrived. World War II reignited the American economy, and during the 1950s the stock market began to regain its strength.

May 1975 began a new chapter in the American stock market. At that time the SEC terminated the practice by which brokerage services received fixed commissions, as they had done since 1792. Now firms could compete for brokerage commissions. The unfixing of commissions also gave birth to discount brokers who, for the first time, could compete with the larger "full-commission" firms on the basis of price. My firm was one of the first such discount firms. After the SEC's action, most traditional firms raised their commissions, but Schwab reduced its commissions sharply. Instead of waiting for customers to place their orders with our San Francisco office, we opened a branch office in Sacramento. The success of that branch office led to more openings, eventually making us the largest discount brokerage firm in the United States.

TODAY'S STOCK MARKET

When people talk about the market today, they're usually referring to the U.S. stock market, as opposed to the international market. More specifically, they often use the term as shorthand for the Dow Jones Industrial Average, one of the most common measurements of the U.S. stock market.

The Dow Jones Industrial Average was created by two reporters, Charles Dow and Eddie Jones, who started publishing *The Wall Street Journal* in 1889. From the start, their newspaper reported financial news and gave compilations of the stock prices of the larger important companies, and it published indexes to track the performance of the stock market as a whole. Today's Dow Jones Industrial Average follows 30 large companies headquartered in the United States. These companies are not necessarily the biggest or the best in the country; they are simply, according to *The Wall Street Journal*, representative of the U.S. stock market. The list of companies can change over time, as a result of mergers and changes in performance.

THE UPS AND DOWNS OF THE MARKET

All this is interesting, you're thinking, except that in the meantime this wonderful, growing, high-performance, inflation-hedging market is going up and down like a Yo-Yo. It may *seem* like that, but that movement isn't random, and it's not a mystery. It's simply the nature of the beast.

Suppose you're on an airplane. All of a sudden the plane rumbles, and everyone around you—your kids, your husband or wife, the stranger in the next seat—goes completely white-knuckled. They're terrified. "What is it?" they're thinking. "What's happening?" Now if you know what's happening—if you understand that the plane is simply coming into some denser air, that there's a wind shear in this direction over 40,000 feet—then you're not white-knuckled at all. The phenomenon isn't inexplicable; it's caused by some force beyond our control. Once you know that, and you realize that you'll soon ride through the turbulence to smoother air, you just bear with it and maybe even learn to relax.

"Bearing with it" is, of course, a little tougher when you're sitting in a chair in your den looking at stock prices, or watching the ticker tape on TV, or just hearing about the market going down as you're driving to work. But the principle is still the same: Once you understand the reasons for all that movement, you're less likely to be afraid. So let's look at some of the causes of stock market turbulence.

The first cause is simply supply and demand. Stock prices go up and down because there's a free market. The price of real estate goes up and down as well, but we don't see that movement as much, partly because the real estate market doesn't move as dramatically, and partly because most of us don't open up the real estate pages of the paper every day and track those prices. Stocks, on the other hand, go up and down because on any given day thousands of investors are buying and selling shares. When there are more buyers of a particular stock, the price of that stock rises because it's in demand. The next week, if the newspaper prints a negative article about the same company—"XYZ's Going to Hell in a Handbasket!"— people will sell the stock. So it goes: One day it's up, the next it's down.

The second reason for stock market turbulence is emotion. Many short-term market movements are unrelated to the state of the economy or the outlook of a specific type of investment. Very often emotion drives the market far more than actual events. The market is deeply affected by the public's reaction to events, and whether those events are real or just rumored doesn't really matter in terms of their effect. Public sentiment alone can send the price of securities soaring or sinking overnight. You've seen it happen: All of a sudden there's word that the president is ailing or a political crisis is brewing, and the news broadcast that night leads with a story about a rush of sell orders. Next comes an overall drop in stock prices. Then some unidentified "they" puts the word out that the economy is brightening, or that there is an exceptional demand for some type of product or service. *Voilà!* There's an increase in buy orders, with a resulting increase in prices.

The market is, of course, affected by real events as well—a third reason for its fluctuations. It responds to all manner of social, economic, political, and business events. For example, the spring of 1997 saw one of the biggest one-day gains in Dow Jones history, in response to news that Americans' wages rose less than had been expected in the previous quarter. That's why it's good for investors to keep up with the news. I find the "Stock Market History Since 1948" chart interesting because it recaps this visually.

There's a fourth reason for the stock market's ups and downs: They simply come with the territory, given the nature of the beast we call a company. When you think of companies as living, growing organisms, the market's activity is no longer surprising. It's not even good or bad, any more than the fact that the weather changes daily is good or bad; it's just the way things are.

The movements we see in the market, both the ups and the downs, have names. Generally, up markets tend to last three to four

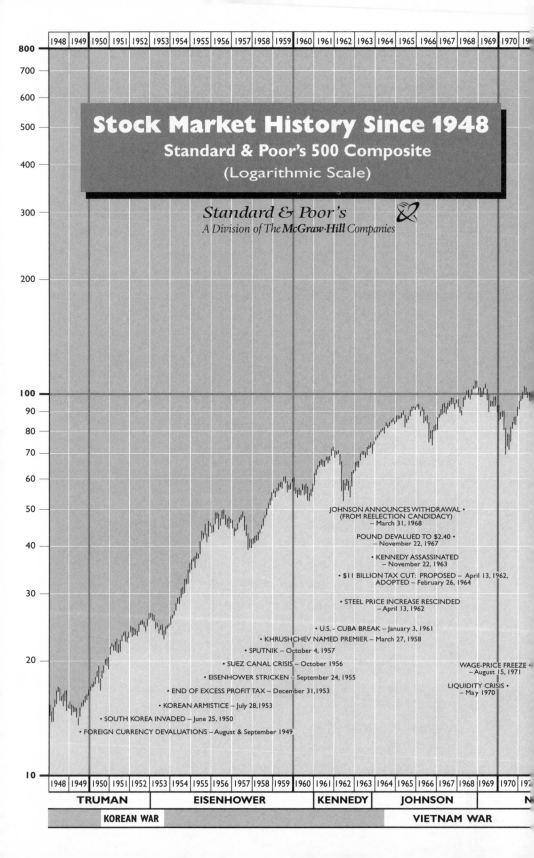

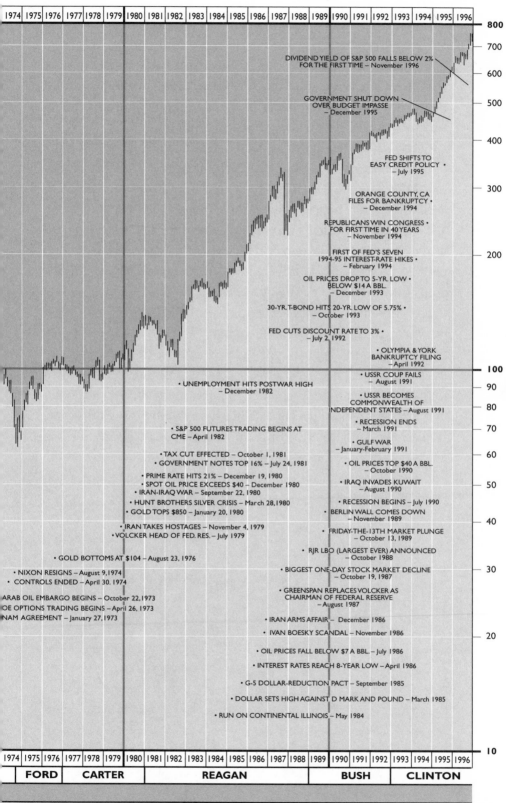

1974 1975 1976 1977 1978 1979 1980 1981 1982 1983 1984 1985 1986 1987 1988 1989 1990 1991 1992 1993 1994 1995 1996

800
700
600
500
400
300
200

DIVIDEND YIELD OF S&P 500 FALLS BELOW 2%
FOR THE FIRST TIME – November 1996

GOVERNMENT SHUT DOWN
OVER BUDGET IMPASSE
– December 1995

FED SHIFTS TO
EASY CREDIT POLICY •
– July 1995

ORANGE COUNTY, CA
FILES FOR BANKRUPTCY •
– December 1994

REPUBLICANS WIN CONGRESS •
FOR FIRST TIME IN 40 YEARS
– November 1994

FIRST OF FED'S SEVEN
1994-95 INTEREST-RATE HIKES •
– February 1994

OIL PRICES DROP TO 5-YR. LOW •
BELOW $14 A BBL.
– December 1993

30-YR. T-BOND HITS 20-YR. LOW OF 5.75% •
– October 1993

FED CUTS DISCOUNT RATE TO 3% •
– July 2, 1992

• OLYMPIA & YORK
BANKRUPTCY FILING
–April 1992

100
90
80
70
60
50
40
30
20

• UNEMPLOYMENT HITS POSTWAR HIGH
– December 1982

• USSR COUP FAILS
– August 1991

• USSR BECOMES
COMMONWEALTH OF
INDEPENDENT STATES – August 1991

• S&P 500 FUTURES TRADING BEGINS AT
CME – April 1982

• RECESSION ENDS
– March 1991

• TAX CUT EFFECTED – October 1, 1981
• GOVERNMENT NOTES TOP 16% – July 24, 1981

• GULF WAR
– January-February 1991

• PRIME RATE HITS 21% – December 19, 1980
• SPOT OIL PRICE EXCEEDS $40 – December 1980
• IRAN-IRAQ WAR – September 22, 1980

• OIL PRICES TOP $40 A BBL.
– October 1990

• HUNT BROTHERS SILVER CRISIS – March 28, 1980

• IRAQ INVADES KUWAIT
– August 1990

• GOLD TOPS $850 – January 20, 1980

• RECESSION BEGINS – July 1990

• IRAN TAKES HOSTAGES – November 4, 1979
• VOLCKER HEAD OF FED. RES. – July 1979

• BERLIN WALL COMES DOWN
– November 1989

• FRIDAY-THE-13TH MARKET PLUNGE
– October 13, 1989

• GOLD BOTTOMS AT $104 – August 23, 1976

• RJR LBO (LARGEST EVER) ANNOUNCED
– October 1988

• NIXON RESIGNS – August 9, 1974
• CONTROLS ENDED – April 30. 1974

• BIGGEST ONE-DAY STOCK MARKET DECLINE
– October 19, 1987

ARAB OIL EMBARGO BEGINS – October 22, 1973
OE OPTIONS TRADING BEGINS – April 26, 1973

• GREENSPAN REPLACES VOLCKER AS
CHAIRMAN OF FEDERAL RESERVE
– August 1987

NAM AGREEMENT – January 27, 1973

• IRAN ARMS AFFAIR – December 1986

• IVAN BOESKY SCANDAL – November 1986

• OIL PRICES FALL BELOW $7 A BBL. – July 1986

• INTEREST RATES REACH 8-YEAR LOW – April 1986

• G-5 DOLLAR-REDUCTION PACT – September 1985

• DOLLAR SETS HIGH AGAINST D MARK AND POUND – March 1985

• RUN ON CONTINENTAL ILLINOIS – May 1984

10

1974 1975 1976 1977 1978 1979 1980 1981 1982 1983 1984 1985 1986 1987 1988 1989 1990 1991 1992 1993 1994 1995 1996

| FORD | CARTER | REAGAN | BUSH | CLINTON |

Reprinted by permission of Standard & Poor's, a division of The McGraw-Hill Companies.

times longer than down markets. A *rally* lasts two or three months, and there are more intermediate movements, with the market eventually reaching new highs and breaking records. The larger up-trend, *a bull market,* can last two years or longer.

Drops in the market are usually named according to the severity of the drop, or how much damage is done. Generally speaking, a *routine decline* is a 5% drop in the Dow Jones Industrial Average. Such declines typically happen around three times a year. A *correction* is a 10% drop, which usually takes place about once a year. A *severe correction* is a drop of 15% or more. We've seen 15 severe corrections in the past 50 years. Eight of them have turned into a *bear market,* or a drop of 20% or more. A *panic* is a bear market or a severe correction that occurs in a very short time, like a period of a few weeks. And a *crash* is a drop of 20% or more in one or a few days. We've seen only two crashes in this century, one in 1929 and one in 1987.

I personally have experienced all these different types of down markets except the crash of 1929, though I learned enough about it from my dad to make me glad I didn't have to live through that one. While down markets are always uncomfortable and always seem to go on longer than you are prepared for them to, as long as you are not overly leveraged you can survive every down market and go on to prosper afterward.

■ ■ ■ ■ ■ ■ ■ ■ ■ ■ ■ ■ ■ ■ ■ ■ ■ ■ ■

OF BEARS AND BULLS

You hear it all the time: "We're really in a bull market," or "It's a bear market, all right." *Bear* and *bull* are names for two kinds of investors and, by extension, two kinds of markets.

At their simplest, *bear* means down, and *bull* means up. The reason for these names? It's thought that they're based on the way the two animals attack. A bear attacks by sweeping its paws downward; just so, a bearish investor expects prices to go down and sells with the hope of being able to buy back later at a cheaper price. A bear market is a declining market, one in which prices are falling because more people want to sell than to buy. Some people believe that the term *bear* also comes from the saying "selling the bearskin before you've caught the bear" because bear investors often sell short, meaning that they sell borrowed stock in the hope of buying it back later at a lower price.

The bull, a more aggressive fighter, attacks by tossing its horns up into the air. A bullish investor believes that prices are going up and aggressively buys in anticipation of a market advance. A bull market is one in which prices are going up because more people want to buy than sell.

ACCEPTING RESPONSIBILITY FOR YOUR FINANCIAL LIFE

When you're talking about long-term investing, the real risk isn't the ups and downs in the market. Doing nothing is a far more serious risk, so whatever you do, get started now. Whether you are saving for that first home, or investing for college for your kids, or planning for your retirement.

A generation or two ago, husbands and wives often divided their responsibilities along pretty predictable lines. Those lines have blurred over the last twenty years, and in many families, finances are now the responsibility of both spouses. There's a reason for that; saving money to invest requires the commitment of both people. Still, we're all busy, and if one partner is more experienced in the financial arena than the other, the temptation is usually to let him or her handle the money. It saves time, right? Why should two do the work of one?

Wrong. This is an area of your life where both of you have to take responsibility. If you're the one who knows more about investing, I strongly urge you to include your partner or spouse in your planning. If you're the one who knows less, do something about it, and take an active role in planning for your family's future. It's essential for you to understand the family financial picture in case of the untimely death of your spouse. Put bluntly, do all you can to "teach your wife to be a widow"—or, if you, as the wife, are in charge of the finances, "teach your husband to be a widower." Take the saying metaphorically: don't let yourself, or anyone in your family, be indispensable in terms of understanding family finances.

If you're the reluctant partner, you may have to push yourself to become involved, but it will be well worth the effort. Ignoring the financial aspect of our lives is a big mistake. When you finally do address it, the task is usually easier to handle than you thought it would be. Gail Sheehy, author of *Passages* and *New Passages*, wrote about the fear many women experience about finances in an article titled "Why Women Fear They Will End Up Living in a Box Outside Bergdorf's" (Reprinted from the November 1996 issue of *Money* by special permission; copyright © 1996 by Time, Inc.) A lot of women, Sheehy says, secretly fear that they will end up broke. For many, the nightmare is living in a box outside a department store. Such "bag-lady fears," Sheehy says, are prevalent, "particularly among professional women who are beyond economic dependence on a man." The phenomenon astonishes her, yet she hears such fears articulated frequently.

It is one she used to share. Only relatively recently did she herself face the financial responsibilities of her life head-on. The first time she earned more money than she needed to pay the bills, she felt paralyzed. She just didn't want to think about how to manage her financial resources. "Now you'll have to learn how to husband your money well," her accountant told her, and she soon found herself the recipient of all kinds of financial advice. An IRA and a couple of individual investments, she saw, wouldn't be enough. She continues:

> It gradually dawned on me that I would have to practice what I
> preach in my recent book, *New Passages*, to people entering second

adulthood: You must be willing to take risks if you're going to shape a new self. So I set out to shape a new "financial self"—not a defeatist bag lady, but an active steward of my own money and an educated partner in joint decisions with my husband.

It meant being willing to expose myself as dumb. I hired a financial advisor. I said to the advisor: "explain it to me like I'm in kindergarten"—and he did. When he forced me to think about how much risk I could stand, I realized that here was a chance to catch up. I had to think long term, socking away a maximum amount of money to grow and compound in a highly diversified portfolio. And I had to ignore the market when it went down.

To my surprise, I found that investing for growth is exciting. It changes the way I think about myself. My bag-lady fears sometimes recur, but they don't control my actions anymore. The best way I know to counteract anxiety is to turn on the lights and face the bogey-man—or, in this case, bogey-lady. Educating myself about investing is the equivalent of turning on the lights.

FIRST THINGS FIRST

What follows are two basic steps to get you started.

1. Take Care of the Basics

Before you invest, make sure you've created a financial safety net that consists of the basic necessities.

Set aside emergency funds. Set aside perhaps two months' living expenses and put them in a place where you can access them quickly and easily—in the event of illness or a period of unemployment, for example. Keep these funds liquid—an investment that can easily be converted to cash. I recommend a money market mutual fund. (This is admittedly aggressive; most books will tell you to set aside six months' living expenses, but it's my view that that's overly cautious and unrealistic, and too large an amount for most of us.)

ake sure you're adequately insured. Insurance is, to say the least,
portant part of your overall financial plan. If you have dependents, health and life insurance are crucial. Life insurance is the best
hedge against that ultimate family crisis, the death of the primary
supporter or the primary childcare person. Inexpensive term life
insurance will protect your family against premature death, and it's
something that every conscientious parent and spouse should consider. Make sure you know the difference between *term* and *permanent* life insurance, which you should avoid. (See "life insurance" in
the Glossary for details.)

*Contribute the maximum amount to an IRA and a 401(k) or 403(b)
plan.* Regularly investing in a tax-deferred account is the best long-
term investment you can make. The combination of compound
growth and deferred taxation has incredible power to increase your
nest egg. I urge you to make this investment a priority in your life,
and try to contribute the maximum. In 1997 the maximum IRA
contribution allowed is $2,000 per person; $4,000 for a married
couple. The maximum contribution to a 401(k) is $9,500.

One way to make sure you contribute regularly is to "pay yourself first" by signing up for an automatic investment plan (AIP). An
AIP allows regular investments to be made through payroll deductions or through automatic transfers from your checking account.
The amount you set aside, of course, is up to you, but I encourage
you to invest as much as you can. Try to start with at least 5% to 10%
of your gross (the total amount you earn before taxes), and increase
that amount if you are able to comfortably. Use that money to invest
for your future.

2. Understand Your Investment Goals and Your Investor Profile

Before you decide what specific investments you will make and
how often you will make them, you have to examine your particular
situation and even your personality. First look at your investment
goals. By forming a clear idea of what you want your investments to

accomplish, you'll be able to put your money to work more productively. Once you understand those goals, you need to understand what kind of an investor you are by considering your time frame and your tolerance for risk. (Chapter 2 will help you do this.)

TAKING ADVANTAGE OF STOCK MARKET GROWTH

One of the great things about the stock market, especially today, is that it's so easy to participate in it. It's like a train in that respect: You don't have to outrun or outsmart it, you just have to get on. And getting on is getting easier all the time. My own low-fuss, low-risk approach for long-term investing (which follows) won't protect you against market fluctuations, but it can help you catch the train easily and quickly.

Compound Growth: The Eighth Wonder of the World

The power of compounding is one of the most compelling reasons for investing as soon as possible. Money that is compounding grows remarkably fast. To many, compound growth is the eighth wonder of the world.

Think of compounding this way: the money you invest grows, then the combined amount of both the original investment and its new value grows again. It's like that amoeba, growing faster and faster. All of a sudden, your investment grows geometrically rather than arithmetically. With compounding, investments that are allowed to grow over time can increase in value surprisingly fast.

A good example is my own IRA. Every year since 1982, the year IRAs became available, I've contributed $2,000 to it. Over 14 years I've contributed a total of $28,000. But as of this writing, it's valued at over $118,000. *That's* the power of compounding—and the power of the American stock market.

The chart "The Value of Your Investment" illustrates how the rate of return on an investment affects compounding. For five differ-

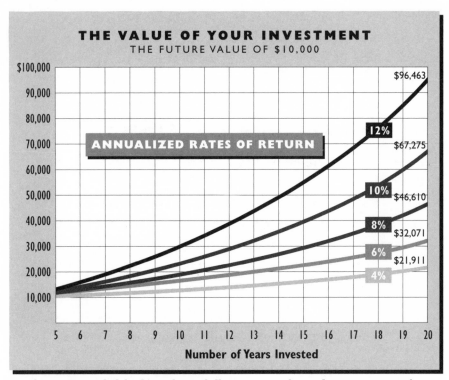

THE VALUE OF YOUR INVESTMENT
THE FUTURE VALUE OF $10,000

ANNUALIZED RATES OF RETURN

12% — $96,463
12%
$67,275
10% $46,610
8% $32,071
6% $21,911
4%

Number of Years Invested

Chart is intended for hypothetical illustration only, and not to project the future performance of any investments. No adjustments have been made for income taxes.

ent rates of return, it shows how much a $10,000 investment would be worth at various points in the future, before taxes, if earnings are reinvested. For example, $10,000 invested for 20 years at an 8% rate of return would grow to over $45,000. The same $10,000 invested at 12% would grow to over $96,000 in 20 years.

THE RULE OF 72

The rule of 72 comes in handy when you're talking about time and money, and it's one of my favorites. This simple formula gives you an approximate idea of how long it will take to double your money at different rates of return. For example, suppose you want to know how long it will take to double your investment at 8%. Simply divide the number 72 by your rate of return. At an 8% rate of return, doubling your money will take 9 years (72 ÷ 8 = 9). At a 10% rate of return, it will take 7.2 years to double your money (72 ÷ 10 = 7.2). And at a 12% rate of return, it will take 6 years (72 ÷ 12 = 6). Don't bother memorizing it; write it down and keep it in your purse or wallet. You'll learn it in time just from using it, and you'll be surprised at how often you do so.

The Safety of Diversification

You know the old saying about putting all your eggs in one basket; most of us have experienced its truth in one painful way or another. We count too heavily on something, and our hopes, at the very least, are dashed when that sure thing doesn't pan out.

Not putting all of your eggs in one basket goes double for investors. As just about anyone who pays any attention to the stock market knows, different kinds of investments do well or poorly at different times. So investing is heads-up ball—you've got to keep your eyes open. One way to do that is to diversify, instead of limiting yourself to only one investment. Divide your money among several different asset classes (for example, stocks, bonds, and cash equivalents), in a sort of divide-and-conquer approach. By mixing things up—diversifying—you can go a long way toward protecting yourself from those ups and downs, and from becoming dependent on any one sector of the market.

William F. Sharpe, a 1990 Nobel prizewinner in economics and professor of finance at Stanford University, gives a simple example: "At one time, each ship sent from London to bring back spices from the Orient was financed by one merchant. If the ship happened to sink, the investor lost everything. But if several merchants pooled their resources, with each taking partial interests in several ships, risk could be greatly reduced, with no diminution in overall expected return. Such pooling could be accomplished in a number of ways. One of the simpler procedures involved the issuance of 'ownership shares' (not surprisingly), with each investor holding a *diversified portfolio* of shares in several ships."

Think of diversifying both among industries—not limiting yourself to stocks within a single industry, such as chemicals or electronics—and among individual stocks. Investing in the stock of only one company is risky, no matter what the company is—including your place of employment. Don't be swayed by emotions, even an honorable one like loyalty.

Mutual funds are a great way to handle diversification. A mutual fund is an investment company that invests in a variety of corporations. Mutual funds come in different varieties, including money market mutual funds for cash-equivalent investments, stock mutual funds, and bond mutual funds. An investor who buys shares of a mutual fund automatically gets the benefit of diversification, without having to buy shares of many separate companies. The mutual fund does the picking and presents you with a sort of investment smorgasbord; all you have to do is choose a good mutual fund. I'd go a step further and diversify among a handful of stock mutual funds as well.

The Wisdom of Matching Market Returns

To be a successful investor, you don't have to outperform the market; as stock market history shows, you can do well if you just match it. Buying what are called index funds is a way to do that, to get in the market and match its performance.

An *index* is a group of securities that are considered yardsticks of market behavior. (We'll discuss them in depth in Chapter 3.) An *index fund* is a mutual fund engineered to match the index for a specific segment of the market. Index funds are very simple long-term investments. They don't try to outguess the market or pick only the hottest stocks. They simply try to match the returns of the index. If you don't want to do anything else, you could invest in a broad-based index fund. I'll go even further: You could put the core of your investments, meaning at least 50% but even as much as 100%, in several index funds. This approach can help reduce your risk by distributing your money across multiple securities, giving you diversification in a number of funds. And index funds are predictable; their outcome is nearly certain, in the sense that they will always match the underlying market.

BECOMING A COMMITTED INVESTOR

I encourage you to prepare for a down market, mentally, emotionally, and fiscally. If you anticipate down periods, you will worry about them less because you will know that, as history has shown, the market won't stay down forever. The U.S. economy is robust and growing, and chances are the market will come back up. I believe it's 100% certain, just a matter of time. If down periods are really going to bother you, you can take steps to reduce your exposure by putting a portion of your holdings into something that won't go down in value. But don't lose sight of your goal in these circumstances, to let the down periods pass. The tricky part about selling is, of course, timing, and not many investors have a knack for buying low and selling high with any consistency. But you don't have to do that; usually you just have to wait the down period out. (We'll discuss tracking investments and learning when to sell in Chapter 8.)

Warren Buffett, the most successful and best-known investor in the United States, says that for him a flip (the time frame for buying and then selling a stock) is five years, meaning that five years is the minimum amount of time that he'll hold on to a given stock. I too have found this buy and hold approach to be more profitable, not only because of that steady overall growth rate of the stock market but because it minimizes taxes and expenses. (You'll find taxes discussed in Chapter 6.)

Holding on for five years can be tough; when you're panicked, selling and getting out can be a temptation. Believe me, I know. But once you've prepared yourself practically—meaning financially— you get better at weathering down periods emotionally and mentally. My confidence has grown over time, as will yours. Remember that investing is not acting on whim, it's not jumping on the latest quick-fix financial bandwagon. It doesn't even stop when you retire. Long-term investing is a commitment, and commitments, as we all know, require patience and endurance.

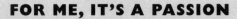

FOR ME, IT'S A PASSION

When I was growing up, other kids wanted to be doctors or lawyers or farmers or teachers. I knew from the start I would be an entrepreneur; my instincts for it were almost hard-wired. One simple reason I was drawn to the business world was that I liked numbers. I was dyslexic (though I wouldn't know that name until years later), and that made other subjects harder for me. Numbers came more easily.

I learned early on that the only way you could make an enterprise success-ful was to find a profitable business idea, do what was needed to make that idea real, then put in whatever time was needed to turn a profit. I started with walnuts. This was in the Sacramento Valley in central California in the 1940s. I gathered walnuts, sacked them, and sold them at five dollars for a 100-pound sack. These were English walnuts, not the black ones, which were more plentiful and brought only three dollars. I learned a couple of things pretty quickly. First, I learned to ignore rejections, the down cycle of my modest walnut market.

Second, I learned that if I wanted to make more money, I had to sell more walnuts.

Chickens were next. When I was 12, I started selling eggs door-to-door, and when my family moved to Santa Barbara, I kept at it. At 13 I owned a couple dozen chickens. The chicken enterprise was more impressive than the walnut selling; it was, as they say, a fully integrated operation, one that took advantage of every phase of chicken farming. I sold the eggs; I learned to kill and pluck fryers for market; and I sold chicken fertilizer. Running my business took a lot of time, about an hour each weekday and two or three hours a day on weekends, but this time I had "employees"—a couple of friends who helped out and shared in the profits.

At 14 I liquidated the business—eggs, fryers, fertilizer, and all. I'd realized that, given the limits on my space and time, I could probably do better in some other endeavor, and while I was somewhat attached to the chicken business and came out with a pretty good profit, it was time to move on. Then I found an even more lucrative and enjoyable enterprise: caddying at the local golf course. Not only did it pay well, but being around expert golfers improved my golf game.

As an undergrad at Stanford, I tried all kinds of ways to make money. During the summers I did various kinds of physical labor—I drove a tractor, cultivated sugar beets, and worked in an oil field, then as a switchman on two Chicago railroads. Later I tried selling—first life insurance, then insulation door-to-door—and found I wasn't cut out for sales. I was introduced to banking by working as a bank teller. Then, while still an undergrad, I found the love of my professional life: I began investing in the stock market.

The point of all this? For me, investing isn't just a way to make a living. It's a passion, something that's been part of me since I was a kid. And it's a passion that I hope has some use: to help other people learn how to plan for their futures.

■ ■ ■ ■ ■ ■ ■ ■ ■ ■ ■ ■ ■ ■ ■ ■ ■ ■ ■ ■

THE BOTTOM LINE ON THE BASICS OF INVESTING

- *Get started now.*

- *Over time, stocks have outperformed all other kinds of investments, including bonds, CDs, and U.S. government securities. It's my belief that of the many investments available, stocks very often give you the best chance for growth over time, and they are a great solution for long-term investing.*

- *Companies grow; when you buy stock in a company, you're buying part of something that's like a living organism. As it grows, so will your investment.*

- *The biggest risk in investing is doing nothing and watching inflation eat up your money. Even at the low inflation rate of 3% per annum, you lose more than a third of your money's purchasing power every ten years.*

- *Mutual funds are a great way to handle diversification.*

- *Index funds offer you a way to participate in long-term U.S. economic growth.*

- *Reinvesting your dividends, instead of using them as income, is a way to systematically increase your investment.*

- *Take the long view, and don't let the market's ups and downs rattle you. After a couple of business cycles, you'll gain confidence and learn to ignore those fluctuations.*

- *Hold on. Investing is not an overnight phenomenon. It's a financial commitment of at least seven years; longer is even better.*

2

GETTING STARTED

Financial goals. Investment plan. Retirement planning. Are you still with me? I hope so, but a lot of people are put off by the language of investing. Some find it daunting, and it makes them feel that they're in over their heads. Others find it as dull as flossing their teeth. As for retirement planning, a lot of folks rank it right up there with doing their taxes—it's about as interesting, only it somehow seems less relevant, and unlike taxes, it seems optional. And it has a sort of nagging quality to it, like somebody pressing you to do something you know you should do but don't want to. You see yourself at the kitchen table late at night, papers everywhere, while the rest of the family sleeps. The questions seem unanswerable: *How old will I be when I retire?* (Most of us don't know.) *What will I be doing?* (Don't know.) *How much money will I need for the rest of my life?* (Ditto.) *And anyway, how much is enough?* (Are you nuts?) In other words: If the train leaves Philadelphia on Tuesday, and you retire in 2014, and your youngest kid has just started college and your spouse has cut back to part-time, *and* you're hoping to spend a little more time on the golf course or the tennis court, how much money will you need? It's as though you're being asked to solve an equation for x when you don't have the value of y or anything else remotely helpful.

But here's a little secret: Planning for your future doesn't have to be difficult. You don't have to know all the answers, and you won't have to stay up all night. So give me your tired, your poor, your exhausted preconceptions about investment planning, and bear with me while I put them just outside the kitchen door and let you in on what it's really about.

Plain and simple, we're talking about *choices*, about what you want out of life. How do you want your life to look? *What do you want?* You know you want "enough." The way to be assured that you get it is to put money aside now. *That's* what's at stake here; *that's* the real issue. And remember, all you're doing is finding a starting point.

■ ■

A NOTE ABOUT TIME

The amount of time that people spend on investing varies tremendously, and you have several options. The least demanding approach in terms of time is to use a financial adviser or investment manager (fee-based, not commissioned). But because of the cost of this service, you should consider an investment manager only if you have $100,000 or more to invest. (Chapter 10 discusses financial advisers in greater detail.)

The next simplest approach is to invest in an asset allocation fund, one fund that matches your investment time frame and tolerance for risk. If you'd like more involvement, you can purchase index funds for each category of your asset allocation plan. If you have the time for more involvement, you might purchase a combination of index funds and actively-managed mutual funds. (Chapter 3 discusses this "core and explore" approach in greater detail.) And finally, if you have the time and energy to devote to research and ongoing management, you could add individual stocks to your portfolio. But whatever method you choose, remember that it's important for you to understand the basics, even if someone else handles the day-to-day decisions.

■ ■

STEP I. HOW MUCH AND HOW SOON?

How do you imagine your future? Do you want to help your kids through college? How about work: Are you nearing retirement or still in the middle of things? What do you dream of: Owning a home? A vacation getaway? Traveling around the world? Maybe you just want to have enough money to keep doing what you're doing now: to preserve your current lifestyle.

What all these goals have in common is this: You need to give a little thought to how to attain them. And that's where investing comes in; it's a tool you can use to make those goals achievable. Investing is what you do now so that you can do what you want later on. Even if you don't know exactly what that is, that's okay. The point is to prepare so that you'll have some financial freedom in the future.

WHAT DO YOU WANT?

You start by looking at your financial responsibilities. For most of us, a big part of that is owning a home. Another big part, for many of us, has to do with our children's futures, a concern that takes considerable planning. (Chapter 9 discusses the effects of a family on investing.) And then, well before our own retirement, our parents retire. We feel personal responsibility for their care, and fulfilling that responsibility can involve a great deal of money. Having been there, I have to say that it's a big responsibility.

Finally there's your own retirement. Even if you're fortunate enough to be in love with your work and you plan on working forever, you still need to have something put aside so that you can slow down if you want to—or if you have to.

A lot of people try to address these responsibilities sequentially, but they can get into trouble that way. Here's what happens: They think, "Well, it's the house first, that's what I'm saving for," so they save for the house and then finally buy it. Then they save for college for the kids, and when it's over, they cross that one off the list. When their parents start needing their help, they squirrel away enough for them. Finally, after they've paid for the house, the kids, and the parents, they figure they'd better start saving for their retirement. They could easily be 50 by this time, and they figure they've got plenty of time, another 20 years to save. Right?

Wrong, and it's a big wrong. The time to start saving for your retirement is when you get your first job, so that the power of compound growth can be working for you from the start. And if you're past that first job, then the time to start is *now*, whenever now is, wherever that finds you. We're living longer and getting healthier, and retirement is getting better and better—but it's also getting more expensive.

Addressing financial responsibilities sequentially simply doesn't work. The easier way, and it's a way that works, is to think of your responsibilities as a continuum. It's not a question of choosing the kids' education over your own retirement. These are both things you want to provide. You don't have to figure out which one to save for first, and often you can't. You won't always know the *when*—when you'll retire, when your parents might need your help—but you do know a few of the *what's*, and you can plan to meet those responsibilities as they arise.

Once you've planned for your responsibilities, you can think about the frills you want—the extras that you dream about before you fall asleep. Maybe you long for a boat. Maybe you want to travel. Or maybe you've always wanted a vacation home. It's possible and desirable to start saving for those as well, by putting aside a little at a time.

INVESTING AT ITS SIMPLEST

There's one simple thing you can do immediately in terms of long-term investing. You can do it now, before you even come up with those how-much, how-soon estimates, before you finish reading this chapter. What is this terrific strategy? *Just put aside as large a percentage of your paycheck as you can comfortably afford and invest it regularly in a broad-based no-load index fund (a mutual fund that's engineered to match the market).* If you do this and nothing else, you'll be ahead of where you were.

This strategy is one of the best around: By investing in one mutual fund, you can be investing in the top 500 or 1,000 American companies. And then just keep doing it, regularly, faithfully. Period. There you go—now you've gotten your money's worth from this book. It's investing at its simplest.

WHAT EVERYONE SHOULD KNOW ABOUT
PLANNING FOR RETIREMENT

Planning for the future involves a lot of variables. Some of us have kids, some don't; some of us want to travel, while others want to settle down. To some extent, your specific hopes will affect how you prepare for your future.

But one part of planning for the future applies to everyone: planning for retirement. But don't let the word *retirement* fool you.

"I'm too young," you're thinking. "I'll never retire. There's plenty of time."

Wrong on all counts. *Everyone* should be planning for retirement, regardless of age, situation in life, or plans for the future. So please, don't start flipping ahead just because you see the word *retirement*. Everyone starts with retirement planning.

When should you start investing for your retirement? The

answer is *now,* and the younger you are, the better. Many successful people today are retiring earlier, at 55 instead of 65, which means their retirement years could even equal their working years in number. Your approach to investing may change as you get closer to retirement age, but the key thing is to be doing it. Even if you're not so young, you still have time to do something.

That's the answer to the *when* question about investing for retirement. The answer to the other big question—*how much*—varies widely, but for most people, the quick answer is, it's more than they expect. If you ask a retiree how much is enough for retirement, the answer is often, "There's never enough."

So how much will you need? How much *will be* enough? Suppose your plans for retirement don't feature circling the world or dividing your time between two houses; suppose you're generally pretty happy with your current lifestyle, and you just want to maintain it. How much will you need? Surprisingly, the ballpark figure most advisers use is 75% of your current annual income, to maintain your present lifestyle.

Where does that 75% estimate come from? It comes from the assumption that your retirement will cost slightly less than your current lifestyle, because some of your expenses will decrease or even be eliminated. For example, you'll be earning less, so your income taxes will be lower, and you may not be paying employment taxes. If you own a home, perhaps you'll have paid off your mortgage or you'll move to a smaller home. Job-related expenses (like commuting costs) will be eliminated or at least decrease. And if you've helped your kids with their college educations, they'll probably be out of school by the time you retire.

Now for the less-than-good news: Your other expenses will most likely increase. The statistics tell us that health care costs and insurance are the big ones. Thanks to more leisure time, your recreation and entertainment costs may also rise. General living expenses such as food, fuel, and utilities can increase simply because you're spending more time at home. Home maintenance and property taxes will usually be higher as well.

Why? Why do we have to invest so much for retirement? There are a few reasons.

First, retirement means both less and more than it did in the past. It means *less* in terms of the financial support you will receive from the government. To be on the safe side, plan on receiving less Social Security, Medicare, and other government support. It's best to view Social Security as a help in your retirement, and only as a help. It won't cover most of your expenses by any means. (For more information, see "Social Security" in the Glossary.)

But retirement means *more* in terms of time and possibilities. Statistics tells us that we're living longer, a trend that will probably continue in the future. Because of dramatic advances in medicine, many of us can expect to live 15 or 20 years beyond our age at retirement. In fact, one anti-aging doctor tells me that if you're alive ten years from now, you can expect to live to be 100. And for people who are living longer, retirement lasts longer. We're fortunate that we may have another 20 years or more, except that it also means that we'll need more money.

Not only are we living longer; we're living healthier. Retirement doesn't mean just sitting around in front of the TV anymore; for more and more people, it means travel, sports, recreation, entertainment— an active lifestyle that clearly costs more than sitting on the couch.

And as always, inflation will be nipping at your heels. The value of your money will dwindle if you're not careful.

So don't be fooled by the fact that you're in your prime and retirement seems as distant as the moon. Retirement planning is for everyone, and the sooner you start, the better.

Fill out the "How Much Will You Need to Invest?" worksheet. The tables should help you determine inflation costs. You may have to estimate in places, or get a little more information here and there. But give it a try; you'll be one step closer to investing for your future. If you're an Internet user, you can do the worksheet online at www.schwab.com/simplesolutions.

STEP 1. HOW MUCH WILL YOU NEED TO INVEST?

Use this Planner Page to help you get a picture of the amount you'll need to invest to reach your goals. The four easy steps will show you the amount you should save on a monthly or yearly basis, or as a lump sum.

Make copies of this page before you begin.

A. DETERMINE YOUR INVESTING GOAL

1. Investment goal

(Enter the current dollar amount of your investing goal)

$ _____

2. Number of years to your goal

_____

3. Inflation factor

(See Table 1, on page 61)

_____

4. Future goal

(Multiply line 1 by line 3)

$ _____

B. CALCULATE YOUR RATE OF RETURN

When selecting your rate of return, you'll want to consider your tolerance for risk. Also consider the kinds of investments you hold. Further, federal and state taxes can have a significant effect on investment returns. Using your estimated rate of return, you can calculate the after-tax rate of return of your investments.

5. Your rate of return

(Enter the rate of return you think your investment will maintain over the period of your investment)

_____ %

6. Enter your tax bracket

_____ %

7. After-tax rate (federal tax only)

(Subtract your tax bracket from 1.00)

_____

8. After-tax rate of return, rounded to the nearest 1.0

(Multiply line 5 by line 7)

_____ %

C. CALCULATE THE FUTURE VALUE OF YOUR CURRENT RESOURCES

9. Total assets

(Current value of assets in savings and/or in an investment portfolio)

$ _____

10. Estimated rate of return

(Enter percentage from line 8)

_____ %

11. Portfolio compounding factor

(See Table 2, on page 61)

_____

12. Future value of current funds

(Multiply line 9 by line 11)

$ _____

13. Amount needed to reach your goals

(Subtract line 12 from line 4)

$ _____

D. DETERMINE THE AMOUNT YOU'LL NEED TO INVEST TO REACH YOUR GOAL

14. Lump sum investment required

(Divide line 13 by line 11)

$ _____

15. Regular monthly investments required

A. Monthly Investment Factor

(See Table 3, on page 62)

_____

B. (Divide line 13 by line 15A)

$ _____

16. Regular annual investments required

(Multiply line 15B by a factor of 13)

$ _____

TABLES

Use the tables below to help estimate your savings and investment goals.

TABLE 1: INFLATION FACTOR

YEARS TO YOUR GOAL	INFLATION FACTOR
5	1.22
10	1.48
15	1.80
20	2.19
25	2.67
30	3.24
35	3.95
40	4.80

TABLE 2: PORTFOLIO COMPOUNDING FACTOR
(Compounded Annually)

YEARS TO YOUR GOAL	RATE OF RETURN					
	5%	6%	7%	8%	9%	10%
5	1.28	1.34	1.40	1.47	1.54	1.61
10	1.63	1.79	1.97	2.16	2.37	2.59
15	2.08	2.40	2.76	3.17	3.64	4.18
20	2.65	3.21	3.87	4.66	5.60	6.73
25	3.39	4.29	5.43	6.85	8.62	10.83
30	4.32	5.74	7.61	10.06	13.27	17.45
35	5.52	7.69	10.68	14.79	20.41	28.10
40	7.04	10.29	14.97	21.72	31.41	45.26

61

TABLE 3: MONTHLY INVESTMENT FACTOR
(Compounded monthly)

YEARS TO YOUR GOAL	RATE OF RETURN					
	5%	6%	7%	8%	9%	10%
5	68.01	69.77	71.59	73.48	75.42	77.44
10	155.28	163.88	173.08	182.95	193.51	204.84
15	267.29	290.82	316.96	346.04	378.41	414.47
20	411.03	462.04	520.93	589.02	667.89	759.37
25	595.51	692.99	810.07	951.03	1121.12	1326.83
30	832.26	1004.52	1219.97	1490.36	1830.74	2260.49
35	1136.09	1424.71	1801.05	2293.88	2941.78	3796.64
40	1526.02	1991.49	2624.81	3491.01	4681.32	6324.08

Assumptions:
Annual inflation rate of 4%.
Investments made at the beginning of the period.

STEP 2. WHO ARE YOU AS AN INVESTOR?

How comfortable are you with risk? It's an important question because your attitude toward risk—how you approach uncertainty—is one of the biggest issues you'll face as an investor. We call this "risk tolerance," and it varies from person to person.

In our everyday lives, we make decisions based on our tolerance for risk all the time. You may be willing to ski and risk breaking a leg, for example, but you may not be willing to hang-glide because the possibility of injury is greater. Or you may be willing to fly in a small plane, but you wouldn't consider skydiving. Where investing is concerned, your risk tolerance means how much of a downturn in the market you can handle without bailing out. How much would your portfolio have to drop in value before you'd sell it all? That's how much risk you can tolerate.

Every investment is associated with a certain amount of risk. There are the possibilities of rising costs, a downturn in the economy, or a sudden upswing in interest rates. You have no way of controlling these kinds of factors. What you can control, to some extent, is the level of risk in the investments you choose.

Maybe you're pretty comfortable with risk; you're willing to risk a little more if there's a chance of greater reward. But maybe you're at the other end of the scale. You're the kind of person who gets nervous about almost any kind of risk. If you're going to lose sleep and be miserable every time the market drops 100 points, you have to take that fact into consideration in your investment planning. In other words, you have to know yourself. Once you know what kind of investor you are, you'll have a clearer idea of what types of investments to choose.

THE ELEMENT OF FEAR

A little fear goes a long way. For many people, fear is the driving emotion in investing—they bring up their fears almost as soon as you mention the word. The idea of losing what we work so hard for is naturally anxiety-provoking. But if that fear goes unchecked, it can really work against you and even become a self-fulfilling prophecy. You lose money because inflation eats it up because you were afraid of losing money if you invested.

A lot of people have taken a chance on the market and lost. They followed a hot tip they picked up at last weekend's cocktail party or tennis game, they invested in their brother-in-law's company, or they bought into a company they believed in with all their heart. Then they saw it fold, and now they figure once is enough. That fear can be even harder to overcome than the fear that results from inexperience.

But the constructive side of fear is caution, and a little caution is a good thing. Where finances are concerned, there are, of course, reasons for caution. I saw a lot of those reasons the summer I was 19. This was in 1958, a recession year. That summer I drove an old Ford across the country to Chicago and applied for a job at a steel mill. There I found long lines of people who were being told there was no work. These people had no hope of any kind of a secure future. They simply didn't have enough money, not that day or that month, let alone a few years down the pike. A 35-year-old musician who had a wife and two kids worked as a railroad switchman, and I mean he worked really hard—with, as you can guess, almost nothing to show for it. For him, putting something away for the future wasn't a remote possibility. He didn't have much good waiting for him in his future. It shook me up, and I saw that there are no guarantees. You have to take responsibility for your future in terms of your financial security, I realized; no one is going to do it for you.

But you can't let fear stop you in your tracks. For what it's worth, half of all the new accounts at Schwab are opened by new investors, which says to me that although everybody should be thinking about investing for their future, not everybody is. If you're not investing now, you're not alone, but start with $500 or $1,000, just something, and keep that fear in check. Be cautious, but don't be paralyzed. When you're paralyzed, you lose out, and *that's* something to fear—because inflation rarely sleeps.

THE ROLE OF CHANGE

Where investing is concerned, it's important to be receptive to change. Once you decide on a game plan for investing, hold that plan in an open palm—that is, be ready to modify it as you change. That doesn't mean moving investments around every month or two; it means reevaluating your strategy perhaps once a year to see if it still suits your goals and your personality. Be open to change in yourself.

Many people find that their attitudes toward risk and investing change dramatically with experience. If you find yourself interested in an investment move that you wouldn't have even considered last year, don't panic—and don't throw the idea out the window. Chances are that the portfolio that took you comfortably from 23 to 43 won't be appropriate when you're 53 or 63 or 73. I've seen myself change a number of times as an investor. As with many things, we become more aggressive as we become more familiar with investing. The more familiar an activity becomes, whether it's skiing or swimming or playing golf, the more aggressive and confident we become.

Like any pursuit in life, the more your confidence grows, the more fun you'll have and the better you'll do. When it comes to financial markets, familiarity breeds comfort and competence, not contempt.

Fill out the "Investor Profile Questionnaire." You'll need your total points in the section that follows.

STEP 2. INVESTOR PROFILE QUESTIONNAIRE

The Investor Profile Questionnaire is designed to help you determine which investment strategy may best suit your needs at this time. The questions address a number of important factors, but key among them are your life stage and your attitude about risk. The questionnaire assumes that the money you plan to invest will be used for a single purpose, such as retirement or saving for a home. Please take a moment to read and answer the following questions. Check the answers that may apply to you. Then follow the instructions carefully. (Make a copy of this page before you begin for easier updating.)

1. I plan to begin withdrawing money from my investments for major needs within:

(Major needs may include retirement, child's college education, home purchase, etc.)

__ Less than 3 years	1 point
__ 3–5 years	3 points
__ 6–10 years	7 points
__ 11 years or more	10 points

Points: _____

2. Once I begin withdrawing funds from my investments, I plan to spend all of the funds within:

__ Less than 2 years	0 points
__ 2–5 years	1 point
__ 6–10 years	4 points
__ 11 years or more	8 points

Points: _____

Subtotal A

Add your total points from questions 1 and 2 and enter here: _____

If your score is less than 3, STOP HERE.

A score of less than 3 indicates a very short investment horizon. For such a short time horizon, a relatively low risk portfolio of 40% short-term (average maturity of 5 years or less) bonds (or bond funds) and 60% cash is recommended, as stock investments may be significantly more volatile in the short term.

If your score is greater than 3, please continue.

3. I would describe my knowledge of investments as:

__	None	0 points
__	Limited	2 points
__	Good	4 points
__	Extensive	6 points

Points: _____

4. When I decide how to invest my money, I am:

__ Most concerned about the possibility of   0 points
my investment losing value

__ Equally concerned about the possibility of   4 points
my investment losing or gaining value

__ Most concerned about the possibility of   8 points
my investment gaining value

Points: _____

5. Review the following list and select the investments you currently own or have owned in the past. Then choose the one with the highest number of points and enter that number.

__	Money market funds or cash equivalents	0 points
__	Bonds and/or bond funds	3 points
__	Stocks and/or stock funds	6 points
__	International securities and/or international funds	8 points

(**Example:** *You now own stock funds and have in the past purchased international securities. Your point score would be 8.*)

(Maximum possible score = 8)

Points: _____

6. **Consider this scenario:**
Imagine that over the past three months, the overall stock market lost 25% of its value. An individual stock investment you own also lost 25% of its value. What would you do?

I would:

___ Sell all of my shares   0 points

___ Sell some of my shares   2 points

___ Do nothing   5 points

___ Buy more shares   8 points

Points: _____

7. **Review the chart showing hypothetical investment plans.**

We've outlined the average, best, and worst case annual returns of five hypothetical investment plans. Which range of possible outcomes is most acceptable to you or best suits your investment philosophy?

(*The figures are hypothetical and do not represent the best performance of any particular investment.*)

Investment Plans	Average Annualized Return (1 year)	Best Case Scenario (1 year)	Worst Case Scenario (1 year)	Points
Investment Plan A	7.2%	16.3%	-5.6%	0 points
Investment Plan B	9.0%	25.0%	-12.1%	3 points
Investment Plan C	10.4%	33.6%	-18.2%	6 points
Investment Plan D	11.7%	42.8%	-24.0%	8 points
Investment Plan E	12.5%	50.0%	-28.2%	10 points

Points: _____

Subtotal B

Add your total points for questions 3
through 7 and enter here: _____

Now you're ready to determine your personal investor profile.

STEP 1

Enter Subtotal A here: _____

This number represents your time horizon score.

Enter Subtotal B here: _____

This number represents your risk tolerance score.

STEP 2

Now plot your time horizon score and your risk tolerance score on "Your Personal Investor Profile" chart on the next page and locate their intersection point. Then find the corresponding asset allocation plan that might work best for you.

YOUR PERSONAL INVESTOR PROFILE

Time Horizon Score

Risk Tolerance Score	3–4 points	5 points	7–9 points	10–12 points	14–18 points
0-10					
11					
12	CONSERVATIVE				
13					
14					
15					
16		MODERATELY CONSERVATIVE			
17					
18					
19					
20					
21					
22			MODERATE		
23					
24					
25					
26					
27					
28					
29					
30			MODERATELY AGGRESSIVE		
31					
32					
33					
34					
35					
36					
37					
38					
39			AGGRESSIVE		
40					

STEP 3. CHOOSING A PIE CHART
FOR ASSET ALLOCATION

You've filled out the "How Much Will You Need to Invest?" worksheet, so you know approximately how much you'll need and when you'll need it. You've filled out the "Investor Profile Questionnaire," and you know your total points. The next part's easy: you match what you need, when you need it, and who you are to an asset allocation plan.

In very general terms, investments fall into three categories: stocks, bonds, and cash equivalents. An *asset allocation plan* is merely a model for how people divide their money among those three types of investments. Stocks, of course, represent ownership of shares in a company. Bonds are like IOUs from a municipal or federal government. You loan it some money, and, in return, it promises to return the full amount on a specific date and pay you interest in the meantime. Cash-equivalent investments are investments that you can easily convert into cash, like money market funds, Treasury bills, and CDs. Each of these types of investment offers a particular kind of return and entails particular risks.

In fact, the two key differences between these types of investments are *return* and *risk.*

Return. Investments offer two kinds of return: growth and income. Capital *growth* results from increases in the market price of a security. Common stocks are probably the best-known growth investment. *Income* investments, on the other hand, provide current cash payments in the form of interest and dividends. Bonds, mortgage-backed securities, and CDs are examples of income investments.

Risk. Different types of risks are associated with different investments. The biggest risk, the worst possible outcome for investors, is losing the dollars they invested. Entire financial industries have been built upon counteracting this risk. Banks and S&Ls tout savings accounts and CDs as "risk free," while government bond brokers promote "risk-free" Treasury securities. But capital loss is only one type of risk; every investment is exposed to one type or another. A savings account, for example, may eliminate market risk, meaning that you probably won't lose the money you deposit in it; but with respect to inflation risk (preserving purchasing power), savings accounts are almost as risky as you can get. Treasury bonds are free from default risk, but not from inflation risk or market risk or yearly taxes.

Each particular investment is subject to all the general risks that come with that type of investment. For example, stock prices rise and fall with the stock market cycle, making stocks as an investment subject to market psychology risk. If you buy stock, you inherit that cyclical economic risk that comes with such an investment. Every bond presents some inflation risk, because a rising price level reduces the purchasing power of a fixed income. If you buy any single bond, you inherit the inflation risk that comes with all bonds.

In addition, each investment is subject to a specific risk that other investments of its type may not have. Every stock is exposed to the business cycle, for example, but not all corporations suffer from complacent management or an antiquated product. Every bond undertakes inflation risk, but not all bonds have equal risk of default.

So you need a way of handling risk. If you try to minimize risk by avoiding what you perceive as high-risk investments altogether, you're really just shooting yourself in the foot. By omitting a whole class of investments, you lose the returns that that class generates. Chances are that a hard-line low-risk approach will produce low-reward results.

A better response to risk is to develop a portfolio that is balanced in terms of the types of assets you invest in. You can think of this as another level of diversification. Yes, you want to diversify within a specific asset group—you don't want to buy only one stock, or stocks in only one industry. But it's also wise to diversify among types of assets. For example, by holding part of your portfolio in stocks and part in bonds, you don't avoid the risk of stocks and bonds, but you cut their effect in half—and you double your sources of return. How you apportion these types of investments in your portfolio—how you allocate your assets—depends on your preferences, goals, and the time available to realize those goals.

Diversification isn't just a good strategy; it's a key to successful investing. Studies show that asset allocation (the way in which you diversify your portfolio among asset classes) is the biggest factor in determining your overall return; *over 90% of your investment return will be determined by the mix of asset classes that you choose.* It's an important fact—don't lose sight of it.

By examining your priorities, your time frame, and your temperament, you can develop an asset allocation that addresses both your needs and your comfort level with risk. As you evaluate your choices, I would encourage you to choose the most aggressive approach that you're comfortable with. By *aggressive* I don't mean that you should be aggressive in making your individual investment choices, or that you look for high-fliers and hot new companies. Rather, I'm encouraging you to be aggressive in terms of the model you choose for asset allocation, within your personal limits.

You won't hear this advice from a lot of financial advisers, but my belief in stock market growth over time is so strong that for most of your prime wage-earning years, I would frankly encourage you to invest primarily for growth—that is, to invest in stocks rather than bonds or cash equivalents. This approach is admittedly aggressive, but it's one that has stood the test of time. While it may sound somewhat self-serving of me to advocate investing in growth stocks, I do so for very simple reasons: my strong confidence in the American economy (as well as the new world economy) and the historical performance of the stock market. This approach is what I've practiced myself, and I've tried to pass it on. If it doesn't feel right for you, I hope you'll check with other professionals. My biggest concern is that you do something smart for your future.

If you decide you just can't handle a very aggressive approach, then start conservatively. You may surprise yourself eventually.

GETTING AS FAR AWAY FROM ZERO AS I COULD

When I was 24, I didn't have much money, and that felt like being pretty close to zero. I didn't know everything, but I knew I wanted to get as far away from zero as I could, because I figured that the farther away from zero you were, the better you could handle loss. Say you have $5,000 and you invest the whole thing in the market. Then you lose 50% of it. Well, you're down to $2,500, not much. But if you have $100,000 and you lose half, that's a big loss. But you still have $50,000; you're still doing okay; you can handle a 50% drop because you're so far away from zero.

When you're young, you're usually pretty close to zero—and I wanted to not just put some distance between me and that zero, but to do it fast. So I invested pretty aggressively—I looked for high-quality, high-growth stocks because I figured that with them I could get farther down the road—and faster—than by just investing in some laggard utility. Today I'd encourage people on the younger side of things to consider doing the same. What's young? Twenty-five is young. Thirty-five is still young, and I'd even call 45 young. Those are the years to invest for growth and put as many miles as you can between you and zip. You'll be glad you did.

What proportion of your money will you invest in stocks? In bonds? How much do you want to keep in liquid investments? Use your total point score from the "Investor Profile Questionnaire" to see which asset allocation plan might best meet your needs. The pie chart you choose will be your asset allocation plan.

STEP 3. CHOOSING A PLAN
THAT'S RIGHT FOR YOU

These examples reflect an established approach to investing—that of allocating funds among different classes of assets.

Bear in mind that the investment plans shown here are only general guidelines. The best way for you to invest will depend on a number of factors, including your investment objectives, how long you have to invest, your overall financial circumstances, your current tax bracket, and the amount you have to invest.

AGGRESSIVE PLAN

For long-term investors who want high growth and don't need current income. Substantial year-to-year volatility in value is acceptable in exchange for a potentially high long-term return.

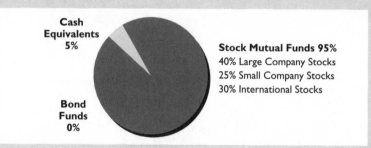

Average annual return (1970–1996): 12.89% Best year: 42.39% Worst year: -23.82%

MODERATELY AGGRESSIVE PLAN

For long-term investors who want good growth and don't need current income. A fair amount of risk is acceptable, but not as much as if they invested exclusively in stocks.

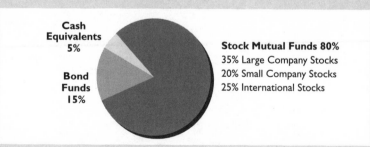

Average annual return (1970–1996): 12.41% Best year: 36.63% Worst year: -19.14%

MODERATE PLAN

For longer-term investors who don't need current income and want reasonable but relatively stable growth. Some fluctuations are tolerable, but they want less risk than the risk associated with the overall stock market.

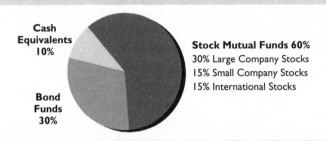

Cash Equivalents 10%

Bond Funds 30%

Stock Mutual Funds 60%
30% Large Company Stocks
15% Small Company Stocks
15% International Stocks

Average annual return (1970–1996): 11.55%   Best year: 29.76%   Worst year: -12.95%

MODERATELY CONSERVATIVE PLAN

For investors who want current income and stability, with some increase in the value of their investments.

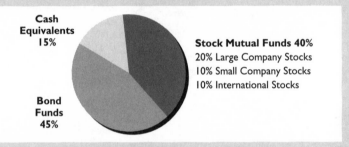

Cash Equivalents 15%

Bond Funds 45%

Stock Mutual Funds 40%
20% Large Company Stocks
10% Small Company Stocks
10% International Stocks

Average annual return (1970–1996): 10.65%   Best year: 25.57%   Worst year: -6.54%

CONSERVATIVE PLAN

For investors who want current income and stability and aren't concerned about increasing the value of their investments.

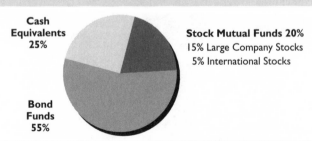

Cash Equivalents 25%

Bond Funds 55%

Stock Mutual Funds 20%
15% Large Company Stocks
5% International Stocks

Average annual return (1970–1996): 9.44%   Best year: 21.81%   Worst year: -1.25%

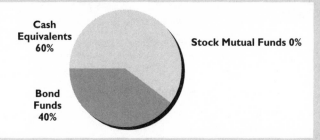

SHORT-TERM PLAN

For investors who want current income and a high degree of stability in their investments.

Cash Equivalents 60%

Stock Mutual Funds 0%

Bond Funds 40%

Average annual return (1970–1996): 7.80%   Best year: 17.96% Worst year: 0.28%

■ ■

THE RULE OF 120

Here's a quick way to remember what proportion of your portfolio should be invested in stocks: Simply deduct your age from 120. The number you come up with is the proportion. The reason is that as you age, you are theoretically less able psychologically and/or financially to handle the losses that might result from a severe bear market. Again, this is just a quick way to come up with a ballpark figure for a long-term, admittedly aggressive proportion.

■ ■

STEP 4. TAKING YOUR CURRENT INVESTMENTS INTO ACCOUNT

Chances are you already own some investments; in that case, you'll need to know how your current portfolio matches up against the pie chart you've chosen. To do that, follow these steps. The "Current Assets Worksheet" will help you.

1. Divide the investments you own among the three asset classes—stocks, bonds, and cash equivalents—using whole dollar amounts. You can think of these as the wedges that make up your portfolio pie.

2. Total the amount in each asset class.
3. Add the three sums to equal the sum of your portfolio—your whole pie.
4. Divide the total of each asset class by the total of your entire pie.
5. Make sure that these three percentages, when rounded up, total 100.

Next you need to look at the stocks and stock mutual funds you own to see how they're divided among large company, small company, and international stocks. The accompanying chart will guide you.

MUTUAL FUNDS CALLED:	FIT INTO THE CATEGORY CALLED:
Growth Equity income Growth & income Large growth Large value Mid-cap blend Mid-cap value	**LARGE COMPANY STOCKS**
Small company Aggressive growth Small blend Small growth Small value	**SMALL COMPANY STOCKS**
Global equity International equity Emerging markets Pacific equity Europe equity World stock Foreign stock Europe stock Pacific ex-Japan stock Diversified emerging markets Latin American stock	**INTERNATIONAL STOCKS**

Complete the "Current Assets Worksheet." You may find that the asset allocations of your current investments don't match those of the pie chart you've chosen. If so, you'll need to rebalance your portfolio. Chapter 8 will guide you.

STEP 4. CURRENT ASSETS WORKSHEET

Use this worksheet to see how what you already have compares to your suggested asset allocation plan.

TOTAL DOLLAR VALUE OF YOUR CURRENT PORTFOLIO

YOUR INVESTMENT PLAN:	YOU NOW OWN:		HOW TO DIVERSIFY:	
	Dollar value	Current %	Desired %	Dollar value
Stock Investments				
INDIVIDUAL STOCKS/MUTUAL FUNDS:				
Large Company	$_____	_____%	_____%	$_____
Small Company	$_____	_____%	_____%	$_____
International	$_____	_____%	_____%	$_____
Total Stock Investments	$_____	_____%	_____%	$_____
Bond Investments				
INDIVIDUAL BONDS/BOND FUNDS:	$_____	_____%	_____%	$_____
Total Bond Investments	$_____	_____%	_____%	$_____
Cash Equivalent Investments				
CDs, TREASURY BILLS, MONEY MARKET FUNDS	$_____	_____%	_____%	$_____
Total Cash Equivalents	$_____	_____%	_____%	$_____

THE BOTTOM LINE ON GETTING STARTED

- *Put aside as large a percentage of your paycheck as you can comfortably afford, and invest it regularly in a broad-based no-load index fund— a mutual fund that's engineered to match the market.*

- *Be a cautious investor if need be, but don't be paralyzed by fear.*

- *Reevaluate your strategy periodically to see if it still suits your goals and your personality.*

- *Learn to keep your distance from the emotional roller coaster of the market's highs and lows. Time and experience will help.*

- *Choose your asset allocation model carefully. Asset allocation is the biggest factor in determining your overall return.*

- *Consider investing primarily for growth for most of your prime wage-earning years.*

II

CHOOSING INVESTMENTS

So now you have a very general idea of how to start. Based on the worksheets and information in Chapter 2, maybe you're thinking about putting your money mostly in stocks, a little in cash. But how do you go about doing it? What are the tools that investors use?

The following chapters will not tell you everything you've always wanted to know about stocks, bonds, and cash-equivalent investments. There are entire books on each of those. Take a look at the personal finance section of your local library or bookstore, and you'll find whole shelves of such books. What the chapters that follow will tell you is what you need to know to get started. If you want more information, take a look at the books recommended in the Appendix.

The "Understanding Your Investment Choices" chart lists various types of investments in each category and illustrates the risk/return factors for each. It can help you determine the right type of investments for you. Consider your time frame and the risk/return relationship of each choice when you make your selections.

UNDERSTANDING YOUR INVESTMENT CHOICES

Lower	RISK/RETURN	Higher

Cash-Equivalent Investments

Investments easily convertible to cash.

- Often referred to as liquid assets.
- Returns reflect prevailing interest rates.

Treasury Bills

Short-term (3–12 months) government obligations. Fixed-rate return easily traded for access to cash. Interest is exempt from state and local taxes.

Short-term CDs

Short-term certificates of deposit from banks and savings and loans that pay a fixed return over a specified time period. Principal is insured up to $100,000 per account—if the institution is covered by federal insurance programs. Rates can vary from bank to bank or region to region. CDs are often available for a variety of terms, but early withdrawal incurs penalties.

Money Market Mutual Funds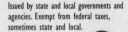

Mutual funds that invest in short-term obligations from corporations and state or federal governments. Typically, it is easy to make deposits or withdrawals. Rates of return fluctuate daily. They're often used as convenient "parking places" for cash between other longer-term investments.*

Bonds

Issued by a borrower, such as a public entity or corporation, seeking to raise funds.

- Borrower promises to repay the full amount, plus interest, by a set maturity date.
- Interest payments are usually semiannual.
- Maturities range from 2 to 30 years.
- Bond value may fluctuate over time, but this will not change the issuer's obligations to pay principal at maturity.

Corporate Bonds

Junk Bonds
Bonds that offer higher interest, but with higher risk of default.

Investment Grade
Bonds that offer lower interest than junk bonds, but with less risk.

Municipal Bonds

Issued by state and local governments and agencies. Exempt from federal taxes, sometimes state and local.

Government Bonds

U.S. Government Bonds
Issued by the U.S. Treasury or other agencies. Exempt from state and local taxes.

Zero-Coupon Treasuries
(STRIPS) Issued by the U.S. Treasury at a discount from face value. Interest is paid as a lump sum at maturity.

Unit Investment Trusts

A fixed pool of investments. May be comprised of tax-free securities, held to maturity.**

Bond Mutual Funds

Mutual funds that invest in bonds from many companies or agencies in order to reduce risk and diversify holdings. Many funds specialize in a particular type of bond. Principal value fluctuates.**

Stocks

Ownership of shares in a company.

- Often referred to as equities.
- May pay dividends.
- Preferred stock dividends are paid before common stock dividends and in the event of a company's liquidation, would receive payment first.

Common Stock Preferred Stock

The market prices for stocks fluctuate with the economic changes, and with the financial condition of the corporations that issue stock. There is no guarantee that a stock will increase in price; you may lose some or all of your investment if the price declines.

Small Capitalization Stocks
Emerging companies, thought to have potential for future growth and profit.

Large Capitalization Stocks
"Blue-chip" companies—large, well-known industrials and utilities.

International Stocks
Stocks issued and traded on foreign exchanges.***

Stock Mutual Funds

Mutual funds invest in the stocks of many companies in order to seek to reduce risk and diversify holdings. Hundreds of funds are available: each offers its own strategy and investment objective.**

---

* Money market funds are managed to maintain a stable $1 share value. Investments in these funds are not insured or guaranteed by the U.S government and there can be no assurance that the funds will be able to maintain a stable net asset value. Prospectuses are available and should be read carefully before investing.

** Prospectuses are available and should be read carefully before investing. Mutual fund share prices and returns will vary with market conditions and interest rates so that shares, when redeemed, may be worth more or less than their original cost.

*** International investing may result in higher risk due to political instability, currency exchange fluctuations, and differences in accounting methods.

Shorter	TIME HORIZON	Longer

3

MUTUAL FUNDS

It's the start of the football season, and everybody knows that come January, only two of those 30 NFL teams will be playing in the Super Bowl, which will have only one winner. So maybe you try to pick the winner. The 49ers have a good shot at it, you say, or maybe the Cowboys, maybe Buffalo.

But if you really want to pick the winner, why not buy the whole league?

You can, in terms of investing. Instead of hemming and hawing and trying to predict which stock or stocks are going to take off, you can buy the whole lot by investing in a certain kind of mutual fund. With one investment, you can own shares in 500 or even 1,000 of America's best-performing companies. Quite a proposition—and quite an opportunity. It's like saying you'll always single out the winner of the Super Bowl; you'll always have the winner in your portfolio, because you own the league.

Picking stocks individually is a lot harder. There are probably 50,000 publicly traded companies out there; that's a pretty staggering number, so let's make it more manageable. Suppose that of those 50,000 companies, there are 5,000 you might consider investing in. You're supposed to figure out—by research or by talking to somebody or by keeping your ear to the ground or by listening to that broker friend of your brother's—which one out of those 5,000 will be the winner. That's a tough assignment.

Now, you may be able to do it. Maybe there are even people out there who can do it all the time. It's just that I've never met any of them, and I certainly can't do it myself.

There is, fortunately, an easier way. You don't have to make a career out of researching companies. You don't have to guess, or hope that hot tip is right; you don't have to pick one team. You can, instead, substantially increase your chance of a solid financial outcome by investing in a mutual fund.

(This is not to say that you can't or shouldn't invest in individual stocks. In fact, picking stocks is fascinating and challenging, and on top of that, it's fun. But it's very difficult to do with any success, so my advice is that if it appeals to you, go ahead—but with only a small percentage of your investment dollars, maybe 5% to 10%, so that you minimize your downside risk. More to come in Chapter 4.)

THE BIG PICTURE

A mutual fund pools the money of many investors and buys stock in a number of individual companies. The fund is managed by a professional who spends 180% of his or her time obsessing about which stocks to buy. By making just one investment for as little as $1,000 in the fund, you can own stock in hundreds of companies. Spreading your investment among a number of different stocks in different industries, as mutual funds do, lowers the impact if one sector goes down. If you find that you're more preoccupied with losing money than making it, a mutual fund may give you a little more peace of mind than other investments. Great portfolios of common stocks may go down from time to time, but history suggests that they seldom stay down for long. And that's not all: With mutual funds, you

can have your dividends and capital gains continuously reinvested,
so you enjoy the power of compound growth.

I've been involved with mutual funds for more than 35 years, a span of experience that includes working for a fund in the 1960s, founding and managing a fund in the 1970s, creating Schwab's Mutual Fund Marketplace® in the mid-1980s, and launching Mutual Fund OneSource® and SchwabFunds in the 1990s. When I first became involved with mutual funds, there were only 500 of them. Today there are more than 8,000. The 1990s have seen mutual funds emerge as possibly the single most important financial asset out there, and they are readily available to the average investor. Today, investment dollars in mutual funds total more than $3 trillion, exceeding the total balances in all banks.

To say that mutual funds are a great way to invest is to put it mildly; in fact, mutual funds, in my view, are the investment of choice for many of us. It's true that the impressive returns of the last few years can't be counted on forever, but mutual funds still have great value. With one investment, you gain diversification that might otherwise be impossible because of the cost of investing in so many individual stocks. In fact, mutual funds are the best way I know of to diversify a single investment. And you don't have to spend your time doing the research it takes to choose individual stocks. A lot of us don't want to make a career out of picking stocks. We already have careers, not to mention families and friends and things we like to do on Saturdays. By investing in a mutual fund, you get the advice of experts at a very low cost, and you're able to make additional investments easily and regularly. All you have to do is choose the mutual fund.

Historically, all mutual funds were actively managed, which means that an individual or a team of professionals picked the investments to buy and sell, based on the fund's stated objectives. Now there are index funds as well, which are passively managed in that they are engineered to match an underlying index.

When you set out to choose a mutual fund, you'll find that an astounding variety of choices is available. To start, there are mutual funds for each major type of investment: stocks, bonds, and cash equivalents. They're known as stock mutual funds, bond mutual funds, and money market mutual funds. Then you go up a level: There are funds of funds, so that you can buy a mutual fund that's made up of individual funds, a sort of diversification-squared approach. And then you go up another level, and you get asset allocation funds. Remember those pie charts in Chapter 2? You can buy a mutual fund that mimics an asset allocation pie chart. Asset allocation funds are designed to meet specific risk/return investment objectives, by including various proportions of stocks, bonds, and cash equivalents.

Impressed? A lot of people are. So where do you start?

■ ■ ■ ■ ■ ■ ■ ■ ■ ■ ■ ■ ■ ■ ■ ■ ■ ■ ■ ■

ONE HUNDRED AND EIGHTY PERCENT

I used to spend what felt like about 180% of my time thinking about picking stocks. I thought about stocks all the time, because it takes a lot of homework to pick individual stocks with any success. And there are no guarantees that your homework will pay off.

But there are other things in life—family, work, vacations, fishing, and golf, to name a few—and those are all good reasons for simplifying your investment approach as much as possible. What is called an *asset allocation fund* is about as simple as it gets. An asset allocation fund is a mix of stocks, bonds, and cash equivalents that is designed to match a specific asset allocation pie chart. First you decide which pie chart fits your needs, and then you choose an asset allocation fund. You're on your way. You don't have to choose specific investments—somebody's already done that for you.

So these days I think about other things besides investing. I think about my family, I think about running my company, I think about my golf game and fishing. You can still have some fun with the market by setting aside maybe 10% of your investment money to choose individual stocks. But that's a long way from letting it take over your life.

A SIMPLE SOLUTION: INDEX FUNDS

With a bit of time and minimal effort, you can pick from a variety of mutual funds and work them into an investment plan. But a lot of people want an easier way. They want simplicity and consistency, they want low fees, they want to be confident that they won't underperform the market.

Enter index funds, which can be a great way to invest, for both first-time and experienced investors. An index fund, as we have seen, is engineered to match the returns of an index, or a group of securities considered yardsticks of market behavior. If the market goes up 20% in one year, so does the index fund. Actively managed funds, by contrast, have a manager in charge who selects the specific investments for that fund, trying to outguess the market. He or she can't always do that successfully. If the manager has a good year, so does the fund; but the same holds true for bad years. Moreover, a managed fund can change managers at just about any time, and often you, the investor, don't hear about the change for months afterward. This can be a problem because when managers change, so can fund style and performance.

Index funds, on the other hand, don't try to outguess the market or pick only the hottest stocks. With an index fund, you don't play the odds; you play the averages, and you're not dependent on a manager's expertise. The objective of an index fund remains constant: to match the overall market returns, as measured by a specific index.

Remember, to be a successful investor, you don't have to outperform the American stock market. Based on its historical performance, you only have to *match* it.

That's an important point, one worth repeating: *You don't have to outperform the market to invest successfully.* In fact, too much money is wasted trying to outperform the market. The low expense ratio of index funds (0.62% annual cost, compared with an average of 1.56% for an actively managed stock fund) gives an index fund a head start in terms of performance.

Another advantage of index funds, as I've said, is their diversification. When you buy, for example, a fund that is engineered to match the S&P 500 Index, you're buying a small piece of 500 companies. When you invest in the Schwab 1000 Index Fund, you're investing in 1,000 companies. This level of diversification reduces the risk associated with investments in individual stocks because your investments will be spread over a wide range of industries and common stock issues. Buying each of those 500 or 1,000 stocks individually would be prohibitively expensive, but with an index fund you can do it with one investment.

Index funds can also be more tax efficient than actively managed funds—a big plus, since taxes are often the single largest drag on fund performance. Index funds tend to have a low turnover, which means lower taxes and, if they're managed properly, little or no capital gains distribution. Index funds are usually no-load (meaning no commission or sales fees), and their average operating expense fees are low as well.

So if you want the easy way out, consider a broad-based, no-load index fund. Such a fund is not intended as an investment for a single market cycle or even a year or two. It should be a permanent, ongoing part of your investment plan (ideally in conjunction with dollar cost averaging, which is discussed in Chapter 7). For what it's worth, when it comes to index funds, I put my money where my mouth is: most of the mutual fund investments I have are in index funds, approximately 75%.

■ ■

WHAT IS AN INDEX?

From *The Neatest Little Guide to Mutual Fund Investing* by Jason Kelly:

> You probably already use indexes in other parts of your life, although you might not know it. We create them all the time to help ourselves compare different values. For example, let's say you are interested in buying a new Dodge Neon. If one of your main selection criteria is fuel economy, how do you know if the Neon performs well in that area? You compare its miles-per-gallon number to the average miles-per-gallon number of other mid-size passenger cars, such as the Ford Escort and the Honda Accord. After several comparisons, you know what is a good number, what is average, and what is below average. Notice that you don't compare the Neon's MPG to that of a Geo Metro or a Chevy Suburban. Those vehicles are in different classes and are irrelevant to your comparison. Thus, in this case, mid-size passenger cars make up your index.

■ ■

THE MEASURING STICKS FOR INDEX FUNDS:
STOCK INDEXES

An index fund is based on a stock or bond index. A stock index is a cluster of stocks that represents a larger universe of stocks. That universe can be the whole market, or it can be a subset, such as utility stocks. The gains and losses of an index fund parallel the gains and losses of the index it's tied to (minus annual expenses). The fund does as well as that index—no better, no worse.

Most general market index funds are tied to one of the following indexes:

The S&P 500®

The best known index is Standard & Poor's Composite Index of 500 Stocks—the S&P 500. It consists of New York Stock Exchange (NYSE)–listed companies along with a few American Stock Exchange (AMEX)–listed and over-the-counter (or OTC) stocks, and it accounts for about 70% of market value of the NYSE.

The S&P 500 poses a few glitches in terms of being a representative index of broad market behavior. Seven percent of its stocks are non–U.S. corporations and investment companies, so it is affected by currency translations. More important, the companies are chosen by a committee, rather than by market efficiency.

The Schwab 1000 Index®

The Schwab 1000 Index includes common stock of the 1,000 largest publicly traded U.S. companies as measured by market capitalization (excluding investment companies), and it represents about 82% of the U.S. stock market's value. I believe that including those 500 additional companies gives the Schwab 1000 Index broader diversification than the S&P 500, as well as the potential for greater returns, because those second 500 companies should have slightly higher growth rates than the first 500, which gives you a little bit of a tilt.

The Schwab 1000 Index Fund makes it possible for you to invest in 1,000 American companies with just one investment. And the choice of those companies isn't mine or anybody else's, the choices are made according to a formula of market capitalization. The fund invests in large and mid-size growth companies, and it's designed to track broad U.S. stock price and dividend performance in order to keep pace with the market. It maximizes your potential return by keeping costs low, and it's managed to minimize capital gains taxes to increase after-tax return.

The S&P 100

Some index funds shadow the Standard & Poor's Composite Index of 100 Stocks—the S&P 100. It is composed of 100 stocks within the S&P 500 for which call and put options are traded. It represents some of the largest and best-capitalized corporations in the country.

The Wilshire 5000

The Wilshire 5000 includes all 5,000 stocks on the NYSE and AMEX, as well as OTC stocks for which quotes are available. The Wilshire essentially takes the entire market as its index.

Some indexes focus on smaller companies, different markets, and foreign countries. For example:

The NASDAQ 100

The National Association of Securities Dealers (NASD) maintains indexes of stocks traded over-the-counter via its automated quotation system (NASDAQ). The NASDAQ 100 measures price changes in 100 of the largest OTC industrial stocks.

The Morgan Stanley EAFE

The Morgan Stanley Europe, Australia, and Far East Index (EAFE) is actually two subindexes of 1,000 stocks traded in Europe and the Pacific Basin. It's the most commonly used index for mutual funds that invest in foreign stocks.

CHOOSING AN INDEX FUND

When you look at index funds, consider the following before deciding:

I. Order a prospectus and read it carefully.

This is a time when you're supposed to read the fine print. Call the fund or your broker and ask for a prospectus, then take some time to make sure you understand what it says.

2. Make sure that the index the fund is tied to is a good match for your investment goals.

Before investing, find out what index the fund is tied to and what market the index covers. Most index fund investors want a fund that represents the general market, so they expect a fund's underlying index to represent "the market" or "broad stock market averages." But maybe you want to invest in a more specific group of stocks—for example, smaller companies with more aggressive growth potential. A fund tied to the S&P 500 wouldn't cover the right market for you, but a fund tied to the Schwab 1000 might.

More indexes are being created all the time to address a larger variety of goals. For example, some blue chip indexes are based on stocks within the S&P 500 but not the whole 500. Other indexes track stocks with low price earnings multiples, stocks of regional companies, or stocks of firms that purportedly operate with an elevated social conscience. The further a fund moves from a plain vanilla index, the more it resembles an actively managed mutual fund, and the greater will be its fees and the higher its risks.

3. Look at how closely the fund's performance correlates to its index.

If the fund is based on a broadly based index, the difference between the fund's returns and the index's performance shouldn't vary by more than the fund's expense ratio. An index fund based on the S&P 100 Index or the S&P 500 Index will probably own all 100 or 500 stocks in its portfolio. The Schwab 1000 Fund contains all 1,000 stocks in the index. But funds based on the Wilshire 5000 might not own every stock in its index. Instead, it will create by computer a portfolio that tracks the intended index. There's nothing wrong with a synthetic index fund if it delivers what you pay for: results that match the behavior of the identified index. However, a synthetic fund's performance should be 98+ percent correlated to its index.

4. Check for no-load and low fees.

The fees charged by an index fund that you are considering should reflect the diminished role that professional management plays in such funds. Somewhere around 0.7% of fund assets per year is the most you should expect to pay. Greater fees imply a spin-off of indexing—for example, switching among sectors of the S&P 500 for superior short-term gains. And a genuine index fund should be no-load.

A fund's operating expense ratio (OER) is the ratio of its annual operating expenses, management fees, and any 12b-1 fees relative to its average net assets. You should consider a fund's OER relative to the average OER for similar funds.

CHOOSING ACTIVELY MANAGED MUTUAL FUNDS

Think of choosing an actively managed mutual fund as similar to buying a new car. If you set out to find the right car for you by examining every car that was available at the time, the task could seem overwhelming. Picture it: lot after lot of new cars, old cars, barely used cars.

But when you're ready to buy a car, you don't consider every car out there, new, used, foreign, American, sports cars, sedans. You consider only the cars that fit certain criteria—criteria that are, for the most part, pretty obvious, at least to you—and that narrow the list of possibilities significantly.

So it is with mutual funds. The variety of available mutual funds is astounding; just about every sector of the economy and every type of investment strategy is represented by a fund. But that doesn't mean, when you're ready to invest in a mutual fund, that you have to consider all of them, any more than you'd have to look at every car. You just have to know how to narrow down your choices.

SOME PREREQS

To start, I have some general guidelines on choosing mutual funds, prerequisites, if you will. These are requirements that, in my opinion, any fund you consider should possess:

1. Consider only funds listed in financial publications such as *The Wall Street Journal, Barron's,* and major daily newspapers.

You want to be able to check on the fund's performance and track record easily. These publications list the per-share net asset value (NAV). The NAV represents the total value of the fund (less expenses) divided by the number of outstanding shares. Many newspapers and financial journals also publish historical performance records of mutual funds.

2. Consider only no-load mutual funds.

A load is a commission or sales fee charged on the purchase or sale of mutual fund shares. A no-load fund is one in which you pay no such fees. With a load fund, on the other hand, you pay a sales charge when you invest (called a front-end load) or sell your shares (a back-end load). (A low-load fund charges about 3%. A regular load is about $4^3/_4$% to 6%.) So by simply considering only no-load funds—in which all of your money will be invested in the fund—you will avoid paying commissions.

I urge you to consider only no-load funds. Brokers or guys on the golf course may try to tell you that funds with a load are the ones that perform best, but they're wrong. Evidence dating back decades shows that no-load funds perform just as well as load funds and often better. A load is nothing but a commission sales charge, and whether it's charged up front or on the back end, it's a significant chunk of your capital. I believe you should also rule out any fund whose operating expense ratio (OER) tops 1.7.

The chart below shows average annual OERs by investment category.

AVERAGE ANNUAL OER

Investment Category	OER
Domestic	
Small cap growth	1.59
Small cap value	1.34
Small cap blend	1.27
Mid cap growth	1.22
Mid cap value	1.14
Mid cap blend	1.18
Large cap growth	1.11
Large cap value	0.96
Large cap blend	1.01

International
Foreign stock	1.44
World stock	1.62

Bonds
Intermediate-term bonds	0.78
Ultrashort bond	0.77
Short-term bond	0.82
Intermediate-term government	0.81
Short-term government	0.76
Intermediate-term municipal	0.68
Short-term municipal	0.59

(Averages are calculated from and reported in *Schwab's Mutual Funds Performance Guide®*, based on data reported by Morningstar, Inc., on June 30, 1997.)

It's easy to spot the no-load funds in the mutual fund tables in the newspapers. They have an "NL" in the offer price column. That means that the fund is bought and sold at the price listed in the NAV column. All mutual funds are traded based on their net asset value. A fund with an offer price that is identical to its NAV is either a no-load fund or a load fund carrying a contingent deferred sales charge. Some sector funds and emerging market funds that require a long-term investing horizon will demand a contingent-deferred sales charge because they want to discourage investors from actively trading the fund. Such funds are exceptions to my rule, and I would pay a back-end load. If you're not sure if a particular fund is no-load, ask your broker.

3. Start with a broad-based growth fund.

When you're starting out as an investor, look for funds that are specifically devoted to long-term capital growth without excessive risk. As you study the performance charts, remember that the funds with the best long-term records rarely appear among the top performers in any one period. By the same token, the top performers in any one period are rarely among those with the best long-term records. Don't try to excel by taking some exotic approach. For now, be content to let the hare go whizzing by, as you place your bet on the tortoise. Unless you're an experienced investor with special knowledge of an individual industry, avoid sector funds, which invest solely in one industry.

For many investors, the funds available through large mutual fund families like Janus, Fidelity, Twentieth Century, Vanguard, and Schwab are good choices. These reputable investment firms offer an ample selection of funds and a customer service network that will make fund investing easier. Both selection and service are especially important if you intend to use switch privileges among the funds in the family.

If you find yourself drawn to funds from several mutual fund companies—as I do—there's an easy way to do that, though it wasn't always easy. It used to be that you'd have to deal with each mutual fund company individually, which took a lot of time and paperwork. I speak from experience; in the 1980s, whenever I wanted to buy mutual funds from several companies, I found it a nightmare. First I had to write or call the fund. Maybe six days later I'd get a prospectus in the mail. Then I'd call them up to tell them I wanted to buy some shares, and they'd tell me to send in the money. Maybe, with some luck, I'd own shares in the fund ten days after my first phone call. And it was even more cumbersome when I wanted to sell. Each month, someone who owned shares in four or five funds would get that many separate account statements. It seemed to me that there had to be a better way.

So I invented what the industry now calls a mutual fund super- market. At Schwab, we call it Mutual Fund OneSource; other firms have followed suit, making everything far easier for the mutual fund investor. You can now choose from hundreds of funds in different mutual fund families and buy and sell them through the same bro- kerage firm. Often you pay no transaction fee when you buy or sell. In fact, you pay no more than you'd pay if you bought the fund directly from the originating fund company. And you get all your fund reports on one statement, which is a big plus. If you use a supermarket offered by a broker, you can buy and sell individual stocks and bonds as well. The mutual fund supermarket concept turns investing into one-stop shopping.

■ ■

THE SMORGASBORD OF MUTUAL FUND OBJECTIVES

You want growth? No problem. Income? We've got it. A little international flavor? Easily done. The mutual fund world has something to offer just about every investor.

Morningstar, the leading publisher of mutual fund tracking information, categorizes funds based on the size and investment style of the stocks the funds typically own:

DOMESTIC EQUITY FUNDS

In terms of size, domestic equity funds are categorized as small, medium, or large, based on market capitalization:

Small cap funds own stocks of companies with median market capitalization of less than $1 billion. Small cap funds also tend to put more emphasis on capital preservation than on income.

Medium cap funds fall in the middle of the spectrum and invest in stocks of companies with median capitalization between $1 billion and $5 billion.

Large cap funds own stocks of companies with median capitalization of greater than $5 billion. Large cap funds also have a tendency to focus on dividend income as part of their objective.

In terms of investment style, domestic equity funds are categorized as value, growth, or blend:

Value funds look for stocks that the market currently undervalues but that the fund manager believes have potential for growth. These stocks are "cheap," meaning that the price paid for earnings and book value or assets is low relative to the rest of the market.

Growth funds are more aggressive than value funds. These funds look for desirable company attributes such as strong earnings, quality, and momentum. The fund manager is typically willing to pay higher prices for these companies.

Blend funds are a combination of value and growth funds. Because blend funds contain both value and growth stocks in their portfolio, they tend to be less volatile than funds that are geared solely to value or growth.

INTERNATIONAL/FOREIGN FUNDS

These funds invest in stocks outside the United States. They usually include international funds as well as regional funds that concentrate on Europe, emerging markets, or the Pacific Rim.

SECTOR/SPECIALTY FUNDS

Sector and specialty funds seek growth by investing in specific sectors of the economy, such as communications, financial services, health, natural resources, precious metals, real estate, technology, or utilities.

■ ■ ■ ■ ■ ■ ■ ■ ■ ■ ■ ■ ■ ■ ■ ■ ■ ■ ■

4. Choose funds with steady performance and a solid track record.

You want a fund that has a good performance record, not only for this year, but over the life of the fund. Consistent performance pays off in the long run. As you look at a fund's performance over time, make sure it holds steady during up and down markets. In the long run, those old plowhorses become thoroughbreds when they pull in a steady 10% or 12% instead of a volatile 35% one year and

7% the next. Look for the median fund, one with a consistent record in good markets and bad.

I pay particular attention to the previous five years because it seems to me that a cycle often lasts three years; there's usually been an up and a down market in that time. So by looking at five years of returns, you can see how the fund has performed in both kinds of markets. If you look at only the three-year performance return, it might lower your confidence in that fund. (Note that performance records are less critical for index funds because we can calculate what that performance is for the last 100 years—it matches whatever the index was designed to track.)

I believe there are "good funds" and "bad funds" generally, but even good funds have bad years. Bad funds are the ones that stay in the lowest quartile of performance rankings (meaning 75% of mutual funds do better), and they usually have high fees. Good funds fluctuate in the top two quartiles of performance rankings, taking only a rare dip below.

5. As always, diversify.
Buy an index fund or spread your investment among three to eight funds.

If you're going to invest in actively managed mutual funds, I encourage you to consider selecting three to eight of them. You want at least three in the interest of diversification, but having more than eight can result in a sort of custom index fund, in which case you're better off with a real index fund. In addition, more than eight funds can lead to some fairly complicated tax considerations. Your eight funds might include a couple of growth funds, a couple of income funds, and a couple of international funds. Or you may opt for the easiest solution: picking one asset allocation fund.

As you read prospectuses for various funds, you'll see the following sentence often: "Past performance is no guarantee of future results." Despite this necessary disclaimer, much of the basis for selecting and ranking funds ultimately involves past performance. Experienced investors have discovered that in any given year, on average only 20 to 30 percent of mutual funds outperform the market. That's why I recommend index funds, which are designed to mirror market performance.

6. Consider a "core and explore" approach.

While using only index mutual funds for the equity and fixed income portions of your asset allocation is both a smart and a simple strategy, there is a modification to this that may appeal to you more. In what I call the "core and explore" approach, you use index funds to form the core of your portfolio and actively managed funds that have the stated intent of outperforming the market—either through traditional active management (like stock picking and timing) or quantitative portfolio strategies—to explore other possibilities. This way, the "core" of your portfolio has the certainty of matching the return of the underlying index(es) while the "explore" part of your portfolio can be aimed at further diversification or simply toward trying to beat the market. An example of this would be purchasing an international index fund that invests in many geographic areas as the core of your international allocation and complementing that with an actively managed international fund that focuses on a specific geographic area that you believe has particular growth potential.

SHOPPING AROUND

Scanning popular investment publications is a good way to become familiar with fund categories and to make a tentative shopping list of specific funds. But when you're just starting out, it's wise to be a little skeptical of them. By their nature, financial publications are drawn to highlight the fund of the moment. Good performance generates publicity, publicity generates an inflow of cash from investors, and great inflows of cash amplify the impact when a stellar fund performs badly and goes into virtual obscurity. I've seen too many investors hop on a fund at its brightest, only to find that it's already a burnout. The top-performing fund for the last three months or a year seldom reappears in the top spot again.

The best source for current information on mutual funds is the Internet. It has the added advantage that you can easily sort the funds by various criteria. (Sources for researching online or with hard copy are listed in the Appendix.)

There are a few kinds of funds that I would recommend you avoid. First, I'd avoid funds that have a guru rather than a philosophy. The fact is that enduring pundits, like Peter Lynch of Fidelity's famed Magellan Fund, are rare. The smartest mutual fund investors, it seems to me, prefer funds ruled by a philosophy. Sometimes a market cycle doesn't reward the philosophy, but when the cycle returns, the philosophy will be rewarded because philosophies have staying power.

It's also wise to avoid specialized, limited-purpose funds unless you specifically want and understand what they offer. Highly focused funds are feast-or-famine performers, doing spectacularly when their restricted investment jurisdictions zoom and dismally when they don't.

THE FINE PRINT: EXAMINING THE PROSPECTUS

Once you spot a fund that you think might suit your purposes, call the mutual fund company or your broker and ask for a prospectus and the latest annual or quarterly report. The prospectus lists the fund's goals, restrictions, advisers, and fees. The annual report shows you what investments the fund is holding, and it reviews the fund's performance during the past few years.

You should examine the prospectus carefully before you invest. There are three key pieces of information you should look for. The first one is the detailed statement of the fund's investment policies, which is found under the heading "Key Features of the Fund." It will tell you what investment objectives the fund is most suited for. Second, look for an account of the kinds of transactions the fund may execute, and the types of securities it can buy or sell. This information too appears under "Key Features of the Fund." And third, look for a statement of the costs associated with buying the fund's shares and maintaining the investment. These costs are broken down by fee type under the heading "Summary of Expenses." The prospectus must also spell out the fund's investment policies, and if the fund has a sales load or charge, it must be described in detail. (You'll find more information under "prospectus" in the Glossary.)

Once you become an investor, you should follow the semiannual company reports. Look at the fund holdings to see what sectors the fund is investing in. For instance, if 30% of the portfolio is in technology stocks, you'll understand why the fund did not perform if technology stocks in general took a plunge. And if you understand this, you'll be less likely to panic and sell out.

■ ■ ■ ■ ■ ■ ■ ■ ■ ■ ■ ■ ■ ■ ■ ■ ■ ■ ■

TAXES AND MUTUAL FUNDS

It's *extremely* important to be aware of the tax implications of mutual funds. The tax considerations for investing are significant enough to warrant a chapter of their own, which you'll find in Chapter 6. What follows here are a couple of general considerations.

Taxes can have a huge impact on mutual fund returns, particularly over the long term. An investment that is suitable for a tax-deferred account (such as an IRA) may not be as appropriate for a taxable account. When you are selecting mutual funds for a taxable account, it's crucial to consider the fund's potential after-tax returns. Two funds that have the same potential before-tax returns may not be equal when taxes are factored into the equation.

If your objective is to minimize taxes, the funds you select for your taxable account should have a way of minimizing capital gains and income distributions, either through low portfolio turnover or a tax-efficient investment strategy. The safest way to identify the tax efficiency of a fund is to check the investment philosophy or strategy defined in the fund's prospectus. If the fund has a strategy of attempting to minimize taxes, it most likely will be clearly stated there.

■ ■ ■ ■ ■ ■ ■ ■ ■ ■ ■ ■ ■ ■ ■ ■ ■ ■ ■ ■

INTERNATIONAL INVESTING:
A WHOLE NEW WORLD

It's my feeling that international investing is a key part of asset allocation, and that every portfolio should include an international component. Every investor, regardless of what asset allocation model they're comfortable with (conservative or aggressive or somewhere in between), should at least consider international investing. It's been my experience that most investors benefit from it—and that it's easily and intelligently done through mutual funds.

The simple fact is that our society is becoming more international and interdependent all the time, both in its thinking and in its business and trading. International investing is no longer the exotic, only-for-the-pros endeavor it once was. It's become commonplace, and with good reason. Look at the numbers. In 1979 U.S. stocks represented more than half of the world's total stock market capitalization. Today that figure has declined to 35%, according to Morgan Stanley Capital International, with the rest of the world accounting for about 65%. That means that limiting your investments to the United States rules out more than two-thirds of the world's economy, a value of over $10 trillion.

Some of the world's fastest-growing economies are outside the United States. Investment opportunities abound in both emerging and developed markets in areas, such as Latin America, the Pacific

Rim, and Europe. In 1997 the United Nations expects the world economy to grow by a sustainable 3%; growth in the developed countries will continue at about 2.25%. But the UN's *The State of the World Economy at the Start of 1997* tells us that developing economies should see an acceleration in growth, from 5.7% in 1996 to 6% in 1997. In other words, many parts of the world are growing faster than the United States.

So just to be a prudent investor, I think it's desirable to invest overseas. There are several reasons, each of them convincing. For one, international investing opens up a whole new world of opportunities. By diversifying your investments abroad, you can tap into the growing potential of world markets. You know how important diversification is in general; diversifying your investments across economies is simply diversification on another level, a global one, and it opens you up to potentially good returns from different markets and products.

Adding international stocks to your portfolio can also reduce its overall volatility and help enhance its performance. Markets around the world are driven by different forces and often move independently of each other. Increases in the value of one market can offset the decreases in the value of another.

Foreign economies don't necessarily mirror the U.S. economy, so when the U.S. market goes down, foreign markets can go up. In fact, there seems to be a reverse correlation between international markets and our domestic market. It's often true—not always, but often enough—that the international market does well in years when the domestic market does not. Despite periods of global recession, this inverse relationship is still a good reason to invest internationally. Compared with a portfolio invested entirely in U.S. stocks, a portfolio composed of 75% U.S. stocks and 25% international stocks has historically produced higher performance, with a slightly lower overall portfolio volatility (according to the Charles Schwab Mutual Funds Research Group, in a study of the 25-year period ending December 31, 1995).

Another reason for foreign investing is potential growth. Foreign companies are often able to grow more quickly than U.S. companies. Though in recent years the U.S. stock market has been strong, the markets in several foreign countries have performed even better. Investing in those markets may improve your chances for better returns.

WHERE DO YOU START?

There are several possible ways to invest internationally. The vehicle that makes the most sense to me is international mutual funds, which offer the most convenient way to obtain diversification. You can also buy individual stocks, or invest in foreign currencies or foreign bonds, but a mutual fund gives you professional management, which is more important than ever when you invest in foreign countries. If you have some in-depth knowledge about a particular security or a specific country or economy, perhaps you'll be able to make sound choices about individual stocks. But if you aren't an expert in your own right, which is the case for most of us, I'd stick with mutual funds. It's difficult enough to keep track of individual stocks in the United States. When those stocks are held in foreign countries, it gets even more complicated. And for the average investor international bonds really don't make much sense, because they're risky in terms of currency and fluctuations in value.

So what are your overseas choices in terms of mutual funds? There are, generally speaking, two kinds.

International funds invest in only foreign companies; they hold no stock in American companies. International funds often specialize by investing exclusively in companies in a specific region (like Europe, the Pacific Rim, or Latin America) or a specific country (like Japan), hoping to capitalize on the areas that will see the most growth. Other international funds invest only in the securities of emerging markets, or developing foreign countries. Their investment objective is usually long-term growth.

Global funds invest in both U.S. and non-U.S. companies, typically putting 20% to 50% of their money in American equities. Now that doesn't sound like much of a difference, but think about it. Say you want 20% of your asset allocation in foreign stocks. If you invest in a global fund without realizing that 50% of its holdings are in the United States and only 50% abroad, your foreign exposure will be far less than you wanted: 10% instead of 20%.

RISKY BUSINESS?

There are complications with foreign investing. One is the difficulty of obtaining reliable information; another is risk.

First, getting reliable information about potential foreign investments can be difficult, because foreign countries don't require the kind of corporate disclosure to investors that U.S. companies are required to give. For the most part, in the financial literature of foreign companies, you'll find less of the information you need to make a judgment. Although some foreign countries are adopting more uniform laws as they attempt to attract outside capital, they still have a long way to go in conforming to U.S. accounting and reporting standards. In short, the quantity and quality of information on specific investment policies and funds varies tremendously.

Second, your exposure to risk is greater when you deal with investments in foreign companies. In addition to the usual risks of investing, you have to consider currency risk. Currency risk is the potential for changes in currency exchange rates, which can decrease the value of your investments. If, for instance, the U.S. dollar grows stronger relative to foreign currencies, the return to American investors in international stocks will be reduced. Conversely, if the dollar weakens relative to foreign currencies, the return to American investors will be enhanced. Currency risk adds yet another layer of volatility to the returns of international stock funds. For example, 1996 and 1997 have seen the development of a very strong dollar.

For those who own equities that are in denominations of a different currency, their returns may be reduced as the other currencies are going down against the dollar.

GUIDELINES

It's my feeling that despite the increase in risk, foreign investing is worthwhile. If you choose this path, keep the following points in mind:

- I would suggest that you invest 25% to 30% of the equity portion of your portfolio in international mutual funds. If you're on the conservative side, you might start with 10%.
- Invest in an international (as opposed to a global) mutual fund.
- Invest in a fund that is well-diversified, meaning one that doesn't have more than 5% invested in any one economy, region, or country.

If you examine performance tables when choosing an international fund, keep the information in perspective. The performance of certain single-region or single-country funds may appear terrific. These very specialized funds invest in only one geographic area (say, the Pacific Rim) or in only one country (say, Japan or Singapore). Beginners beware: Funds restricted to a single region are riskier than diversified international funds because they're more volatile—and single-country funds are more volatile still. The reason is simple. If the region or country suffers a crisis or economic blow, many of its stocks are likely to suffer.

A TALE OF TEN FUNDS

A few years ago, a friend of mine found he was tired of trying to pick the top few mutual funds, so he decided to really diversify. He went out and bought ten funds, putting the same dollar amount in each fund. They weren't sector funds; they were good solid funds with five-year track records. Two years passed, then three, and guess what happened? They all did well; some did a little better, some did a little worse, but all ten came within a small percentage of one another. And the average hit the index almost on the nose. My friend's group of ten funds had done just about exactly what all the experts predict happens when someone buys a whole array of the top-performing funds; he ended up with an index fund. Essentially, he had made his own index.

In the end he wound up selling them all. Why? The bookkeeping was a nightmare. Keeping track of ten separate funds—the dividends, the taxes, reinvestment (which creates a new tax basis)—just about drove him nuts. Finally he looked at it all and said, "This is crazy." After he sold them all, he reinvested in an index fund, which is giving him what he wanted in the first place: diversification, tax advantages, one statement that tells him everything he needs to know about his investments, and lower expenses.

THE BOTTOM LINE ON MUTUAL FUNDS

- *To be a successful investor, you don't have to outperform the market; you only have to match it.*

- *I consider mutual funds to be the investment of choice for many of us. With one investment, you get diversification that might otherwise be impossible.*

- *No-load mutual funds are about the best investment you can make for an IRA.*

- *Index funds can be a great way to invest, for both first-time and experienced investors.*

- *Consider only funds that are listed in reputable financial publications.*

- *Consider only no-load mutual funds.*

- *Look for funds that have good performance records, not only for this year but over the life of the fund.*

- *A good way to diversify is to use a "core and explore" approach. You use index funds to form the core of your portfolio and selectively add actively managed funds for further diversification or to try to beat the market.*

- *Unless you're an experienced investor, avoid sector funds.*

- *The best source I know of for timely fund information is the Internet.*

- *With mutual funds, as with other investments, the higher the risk, the greater the potential reward.*

- *Taxes can have a huge impact on mutual fund returns. Check the investment philosophy or strategy defined in the fund's prospectus. An investment that is suitable for a tax-deferred account (such as an IRA) may not be as appropriate for a taxable account.*

- *It's my feeling that international investing is a key part of asset allocation, and that every portfolio should include an international component.*

4

INDIVIDUAL STOCKS

It's great to be able to buy the whole league—to invest in an index mutual fund. But trying to spot an individual winner can be pretty exciting stuff, and that's one of the appeals of buying individual stocks—you're out to pick a winner. You just never know what's going to emerge out there. What new product will be introduced? How will the company grow? How will it do in the marketplace compared to its competitors? You see something that you think has potential, you track it for a while and do your homework, and then maybe you get to the point where you're ready to say, "That's the one!" And who knows? You might just be right. Picking a winner is one of the greatest feelings in the world. It can be a lot of fun, and it can be rewarding as well, both psychologically and financially. But don't kid yourself: if you go down that path, you'll probably hit more bumps than someone who plays it a little safer.

What's involved in picking a winner? Not guesswork. Not whims. You're not just buying a lottery ticket. You have to bring experience and analysis to the vast world of individual stocks. I'm a great believer in buying individual stocks, as long as you do it carefully and in moderation. It is, of course, riskier than mutual fund investing, and it takes more time. But it can be done, and done wisely.

Common stocks are actual shares of ownership in a company. They are classified in three broad groups. *Blue-chip* stocks are shares in typically large, well-established companies. *Growth* stocks are shares in companies with the potential for strong earnings growth. *Small company* stocks are shares in companies that have a comparatively small total market value.

Each type of stock offers different potential for return and corresponding risks. Blue chips, for example, have established performance histories and generally carry less risk. Small company stocks may have greater growth potential and higher possible returns, but they are also much more volatile. Generally speaking, a higher return involves a higher risk.

When you invest in common stock, you're essentially participating in company ownership. Whether you win or lose on your investment depends on the success or failure of that company over time. The more successful the company is, the better the chance for a good return on your money. The less successful it is, the greater your chance of a loss.

The idea of ownership is an important one. Suppose you own stock in Fun & Games, Inc. That means you're part owner of that company. When you go down to the Fun & Games store and buy your kids a bunch of toys, you can feel really great because you own a small piece of that company. You're even helping it grow by shopping there. Or maybe you visit it and you're less than wildly enthusiastic about the way things are being run. Well, you can do something about it. You can sell your stock if the trend continues.

Stocks of established corporations are usually safer than stocks of young, unproven firms, although even "proven" companies can suffer setbacks. But because they will have a track record, you can evaluate them more knowledgeably. Small companies, on the other hand, may have explosive growth potential but no track record. That is, in part, why investments in these stocks are usually considered high risk.

THE BASICS

As a start, I'll lay down some ground rules for individual stock investing. We'll discuss them more fully later in this chapter.

Don't invest more than 10% of your total pot in any one stock.

It's wise to keep the core of your investment pot in mutual funds, then set aside a specific amount to invest in individual stocks.

Get to know the company.

Say you hear about a company that appeals to you. What are the first steps you take? The standard approach is to get all the information you can about it, and that takes time. It also takes a little experience and know-how to be able to analyze all that information. There's no hurry, so don't make the mistake of bypassing the research just to get in quick. This rule may sound obvious, but a lot of people either don't research at all or they stop researching too early.

Buy stock only in companies that you'll want to hold on to.

Remember that investing has a connection to your real life; don't buy into a company that you can't stand or whose policies you disagree with.

Buy what you know.

A lot of investors wisely limit the individual stocks they invest in to industries that they're familiar with. Buy stocks you know about, either through your work or through some other kind of experience. Unless you really love to do research, the kind of research that's necessary to really get to know a company is hard to do.

Ease in.

Suppose you're ready to invest $2,000 in individual stocks. Decide on four or more stocks that look promising, and purchase an equal dollar amount of each. Don't worry if your money doesn't buy a round lot (100 shares). Start out with the same dollar amount in each stock and monitor the results, then add to the investments that perform well and replace those that fall behind. When you add new money, you can use it to buy additional shares of the same stocks or new ones. When you have ten or twelve stocks, you'll be close to the number that most people can manage comfortably. If you're investing in only individual stocks and don't have index or actively managed mutual funds in your portfolio, be sure to diversify among industries to spread your risk.

Take your time.

If a stock is fundamentally sound, you have plenty of time to buy it. The stock market is not a bargain basement. If a stock looks good today, you don't have to act on it this afternoon. If it's a good buy for the long term, you can wait a month, or six, before investing in it.

Experience can be a great teacher;
the more experience you have, the better you get.

As you gain experience, you learn to sense broad movements in the market. Buying individual stocks isn't a onetime experience; like the rest of investing, it's a long-term affair. So be ready to learn from both your successes and your mistakes, and you'll be better off in the long run.

ADVICE FROM A MASTER: WARREN BUFFETT ON INVESTING

Most investors, both institutional and individual, will find that the best way to own common stocks is through an index fund that charges minimal fees. Those following this path are sure to beat the net results (after fees and expenses) delivered by the great majority of investment professionals.

Should you choose, however, to construct your own portfolio, there are a few thoughts worth remembering. Intelligent investing is not complex, though that is far from saying that it is easy. What an investor needs is the ability to correctly evaluate selected businesses. Note that word "selected": You don't have to be an expert on every company, or even many. You only have to be able to evaluate companies within your circle of competence. The size of that circle is not very important; knowing its boundaries, however, is vital.

Your goal as an investor should simply be to purchase, at a rational price, a part interest in an easily understandable business whose earnings are virtually certain to be materially higher five, ten, and twenty years from now. Over time, you will find only a few companies that meet these standards—so when you see one that qualifies, you should buy a meaningful amount of stock. You must also resist the temptation to stray from your guidelines: If you aren't willing to own a stock for ten years, don't even think about owning it for ten minutes. Put together a portfolio of companies whose aggregate earnings march upward over the years, and so also will the portfolio's market value.

Our portfolio shows little change: We continue to make more money when snoring than when active.

Inactivity strikes us as intelligent behavior. Neither we nor most business managers would dream of feverishly trading highly-profitable subsidiaries because a small move in the Federal Reserve's discount rate was predicted or because some Wall Street pundit had reversed his views on the market. Why, then, should we behave differently with our minority positions in wonderful businesses? The art of investing in public companies successfully is little different from the art of successfully acquiring subsidiaries. In each case you simply want to acquire, at a sensible price, a business with excellent economics and able, honest management. Thereafter, you need only monitor whether these qualities are being preserved.

When carried out capably, an investment strategy of that type will often result in its practitioner owning a few securities that will come to represent a very large portion of his portfolio. This investor would get a similar result if he followed a policy of purchasing an interest in, say, 20 percent of the future earnings of a number of outstanding college basketball stars. A handful of these would go on to achieve NBA stardom, and the investor's take from them would soon dominate his royalty stream. To suggest that this investor should sell off portions of his most successful investments simply because they have come to dominate his portfolio is akin to suggesting that the Bulls trade Michael Jordan because he has become so important to the team.

■ ■ ■ ■ ■ ■ ■ ■ ■ ■ ■ ■ ■ ■ ■ ■ ■ ■ ■

INITIAL PUBLIC OFFERINGS

An initial public offering (IPO), or a new issue, is a private company whose shares are being offered to the public for the first time. That first offering is sometimes accompanied by a lot of media attention and excitement. Remember Netscape? Its stock price doubled during its first week of public trading. If you're interested in and excited about a new issue, my suggestion is to go slow, despite the hype. Get the prospectus, and be patient. Check out the company in the same way you would any other company. Keep an eye on the stock, and buy it if and only if you're still interested and it meets your investing objectives, *once the price has stabilized.*

■ ■ ■ ■ ■ ■ ■ ■ ■ ■ ■ ■ ■ ■ ■ ■ ■ ■ ■

CHOOSING INDIVIDUAL STOCKS

How do you choose which stock to invest in? There are lots of approaches to spotting stocks that may have potential. Basically I look for a healthy, thriving company—one that's doing well financially, with consistent earnings and reasonable debt. I look at its business. Does it create sustainable revenues? Does it put the customer first by listening, understanding, and serving? Is management quick and adaptable? Does it create a product that more and more people will use? Is its product contemporary? Who's the competition? And, of course, I look at performance. What's the trend of earnings? Of the stock price? These questions help me identify growth.

Just paying attention to the world you live in is a great way to start. When I took my kids to Disneyland in 1963, I knew nothing about Disney as a company, but Disneyland was filled with more people than some towns I'd visited. I didn't need a brokerage report to tell me what that meant. My kids talked me into trying McDonald's in 1968, and what caught my attention, more than the hamburger I ate, was the sign under the golden arches tallying the millions who'd been served. You don't have to be a wizard to figure what happens to stocks of companies that sell millions of their product. Toys 'R' Us was another one. The first time I walked in, the place was gaga with parents and kids and clerks ringing sales as fast as they could run the registers.

Another way to discover good individual growth stocks is to observe how our culture's needs and tastes are changing. Changes mean that new goods and services must be provided. During the 1950s, for example, a postwar boom unleashed a demand for housing, automobiles, and consumer goods. As a result, stocks of heavy industry, automakers, and manufacturers of consumer products performed well. In the 1990s we can discern some clear trends. One is the rapid growth of the older population, which means that stocks of medical care services, nursing homes, and pharmaceutical companies could do well. This is also the age of heightened environmental awareness, so companies that clean up dump sites, restore ravaged ecologies, and engage in waste recycling may grow. Another area of opportunity is the newly democratized countries of Eastern Europe. These heavy centers of population lack many of the basic goods and services that we take for granted. High-tech, telecommunications, automotive, and other U.S. and multinational firms are moving fast to carve out a market share there.

You might spot a trend that's far more subtle than these. Notice how personal preferences are shifting, and then look for the issues that could cash in. One good place for trend-spotting is newspaper and magazine ads. By observing who's *selling* what, you're also observing who's *buying* what.

And you can watch for "product stocks," or stocks of a company with a hot product or service, the sales of which drive revenues and stock price skyward. The product can be anything, even a service like 24-hour package delivery worldwide. Hundreds of stocks have been rocketed by a single product: Cabbage Patch Kids and Teenage Mutant Ninja Turtles, Velcro and The Pump, personal computers, contact lenses and laparoscopes and Rogaine, Disney World, the Mustang fastback and the Mazda Miata, cellular phones, pet rocks, button-fly jeans, and Tomahawk missiles.

Product stocks are associated with technological advances, changing consumer tastes, and great marketing. But those very circumstances can also destroy them, and that's where you can run into problems. Product stocks have to sustain their magic to sustain their growth. If the product doesn't have legs, the stock's run will be short. The company has to sustain that product through refinements, improvements, and product-cycle extensions. That's what growth investors look for in product stocks.

Finally, I like to watch the small companies, meaning firms with market capitalization of less than $500 million (the number of shares outstanding multiplied by price per share). Sometimes small companies are defined as those with less than $200 million in sales or with stocks selling under $10 a share. The appeal of a small growing company with fewer shares is obvious: A relatively small increment of new revenue can add dramatically to earnings per share (the total earnings for a period divided by the number of shares outstanding) and stock price.

Investors often spot promising small companies in *Fortune*'s annual issue highlighting America's 100 fastest-growing companies. Others subscribe to newsletters that follow small company stocks. But with small companies, you must be particular and willing to tolerate giant price fluctuations. If you invest for the "small firm effect," consider a small company mutual fund. But choosing the right small company fund is more difficult than choosing a large fund, so do your homework.

■ ■

SOME COOL ADVICE
ON HOT TIPS

Hot tips: snippets of conversation overheard at cocktail parties or on the golf course about how XYZ Co. is about to get really big. Hot tips can be tempting, but after 40 years of experience, I can tell you this with certainty: They just aren't worth it. I've never had anybody tell me, "Hey, I sure am glad I followed that hot tip I got! Boy, did it pay off!" It just doesn't happen. What does happen is the opposite. You end up kicking yourself, and saying, "What was I thinking?"

What we're talking about is speculation, guesswork really, and part of the attraction of speculation is simply human nature. Watch someone dropping quarters in a slot machine. They get a little thrill every time they pull the crank because they figure, "You never know."

Exactly, you don't know. But why put your money someplace when you don't know? Human nature being what it is, sometimes we just have to try something in order to be convinced; there's just no other way. Maybe touching this particular hot stove once is the only way you'll learn to avoid it.

The problem is, that's how some people see investing: as just another game of chance, like the casino, the racetrack, the lottery. To them, it's all the same. Too many investors rely on luck, with their philosophy and preparation amounting to no more than "I hope this stock pays off." But even if lightning strikes and somehow, against the odds, they manage to choose a good stock, they'll lack the understanding and discipline to hold it until it pays off.

These people don't see how serious investing is. But you know different; you know that throwing money after a hot tip isn't investing. It's gambling, plain and simple, and the two are worlds apart.

So if you've got those take-a-shot-at-it urges coursing through your blood, go buy a lottery ticket. Or hop on a plane to Las Vegas, and have a great time. Get it out of your system if you have to, but don't act on it by investing in stocks. And if you really, really, really have to follow a hot tip—if you hear about something, and you just cannot rest until you check it out—at least do it carefully. Keep the dollar amount small. And when you lose the money, walk away from the loss, but don't walk away from investing.

■ ■ ■ ■ ■ ■ ■ ■ ■ ■ ■ ■ ■ ■ ■ ■ ■ ■ ■ ■

CHECKING THE FINE PRINT: EVALUATING STOCKS

Once you find one or more stocks that look interesting, follow their activity in the paper. You might also use some of the resources listed in the Appendix to do a little research. I like to check how much of the company is owned by its management. In my mind, the higher the percentage, the better, with 10% the minimum. I also look at how the stock has performed relative to an index such as the Schwab 1000 or the S&P 500. And of course I look at the fundamentals:

Quality

The quality of a stock can be measured in a number of ways, but probably the most popular is the company's earnings trend. A company's earnings are its net income or profit, often called its bottom line. Since company earnings usually show up in millions of dollars, it's handy to break that figure down to a smaller number, called *earnings per share* (EPS).

Earnings per share is derived by dividing the company's total earnings for a period by the number of shares outstanding. Fifty million dollars in earnings and 20 million shares outstanding would put earnings at $2.50 on a per-share basis. That $2.50 EPS has meaning only if it can be compared with earlier-reported EPS figures. You may be able to forgive a downturn in a year or a quarter due to special company problems or general economic change, but ideally you expect an earnings improvement, an uptrend, over time.

Strong earnings momentum is likely to be shown by younger, growing companies. More established quality companies will make slight improvements over various quarters, but it's more likely to be branded as a company with "stable earnings." There's nothing wrong with stability.

As a young investor, I used to search for companies with accelerating earnings by circling earnings announcements in *The Wall Street Journal.* Today stocks are routinely ranked by comparing earnings to expectations and historical trends. The principle is the same: Buy stock in companies with accelerated earnings early, and hope the trend continues.

Stocks with improved earnings and accelerated prices are momentum stocks, and they're solid investments while earnings outpace price. William J. O'Neil popularized momentum investing through his newspaper, *Investor's Business Daily.* Its stock tables rank earnings per share growth, relative price strength, and other information for momentum strategists.

Value in the Market

Buying stock at a good value is like purchasing anything else at a bargain price. Overall return from a growth stock can be greatly enhanced by paying a price that's currently under historic levels for that stock.

It would be easy to think that the chief yardstick of a company's value is the price of its stock, but it's not. The price of the stock is more an indication of the public's current opinion of the company. On any given day, the public votes on a company or gives it a performance appraisal, in a very tangible way: with their money. If they have faith in the company, they buy; if they don't, they sell.

The chief yardstick of a company's value is its price/earnings ratio (P/E). This ratio represents the relationship between the price of the stock and its earnings for the past year. To figure it, you divide the current price by the earnings per share for that year. A $20 stock that earns $2 per share has a P/E of 10 ($20 divided by $2). So for $10, you're buying $1 of earnings per share. The P/E is also called the "multiple." At a 10 P/E, a company is selling at a multiple of 10 times its earnings.

When you scan the financial pages, you'll see a range of P/Es, some as low as 0.5 and others above 100. There is no set rule on what's a good P/E, but generally a low P/E is a good sign because it often means that the price has not risen to reflect the company's earnings ability, so the stock may be undervalued. A high P/E, on the other hand, could be the result of either a runaway price or depressed earnings. Both are red flags. Be particularly wary of faddish or trendy stocks, such as high-flying high-tech or biotech stocks. It's easy for buyers to get excited over front-page news. As they blindly join the parade, the prices of these stocks can leap far ahead of earnings. Many of them ultimately crash.

One factor in assessing a company's P/E is its stage of development. A new company passes through a development stage characterized by a high P/E. It may have no earnings for years, yet its stock may move higher as investors anticipate earnings. Then the company may enter the aggressive-growth stage, marked by strong year-to-year earnings gains. Earnings growth and P/E accelerate until the company exhausts its market, or competition erodes market share.

YOU GET WHAT YOU PAY FOR: PENNY STOCKS

Penny stocks are stocks that sell for five dollars or less. They're attractive to people in the same way that slot machines are attractive: You don't have to put much on the table, and you think you really might hit it big.

The problem is that when you buy penny stocks, you're seldom buying quality, and that's crucial in stocks. So why not buy quality? Penny stocks usually have no new revenues, no income, and no capital—that's why they're penny stocks. I put them in the hot tip category. People don't usually get into penny stocks for solid reasons; they do it because they're acting on a hunch, and it looks like easy money.

But if you ranked companies by quality, penny stocks would be right down at the bottom. They have the worst quality you can think of and the highest potential for loss. Why invest in that? Go for quality. I've come to appreciate quality more as I've gotten older, whether we're talking about art or jewelry or real estate. It's so easy to buy quality stocks at incredibly efficient prices; why even consider garbage?

A wait-and-see approach is a good idea for penny stocks. If it's a fundamentally good company, wait until it hits ten dollars. Let it prove itself a little before you jump in.

Every successful company outlives its aggressive-growth stage. The company's earnings may continue to rise, but its P/E will decline as the market reevaluates an acceptable price for the company's future profits. Earnings growth also slows as the company gets bigger; it's hard for bigger companies to repeat big percentage earnings increases. A financially strong, mature company may become a blue-chip stock, but it will sell at a lower P/E than companies likely to show accelerated growth.

Dividends

A dividend is an individual's share of any profits that a company distributes to its shareholders. Companies typically declare and pay dividends quarterly. Always weigh a stock in terms of its total return: both growth (price per share) and income (dividends). The *dividend yield* is the annual dividend divided by the current price.

An income-oriented investor will seek a stock with a high dividend yield that rises steadily over time, while a growth stock investor will look for a stock with a lower but steadily growing dividend. Such an investor wants the dividend to grow because a growing dividend indicates that the company is fundamentally strong and should turn in a good long-term performance. High-growth companies typically pay very low dividends (which wise investors reinvest to take advantage of compound growth) or no dividends at all (since they reinvest most of their profits back into the company for growth).

 Higher dividends mean higher current taxes. Growth stock investors don't like that. They're looking for an *unrealized* capital gain, which means a gain (growth in share price) that isn't taxed until the stock is sold.

SEEING WITH INVESTOR'S EYES

Once you start investing—or even *considering* investing—your horizons broaden. Investing is a pretty interesting phenomenon, and an organic one at that. And watching it isn't all that different from watching a sporting event.

When I started investing, I became something of a news hog. I couldn't help thinking of current events in terms of their effect on the economy: What would the next election do to the market? The president's trip to China? The announcement of a high-tech merger? Soon I found myself looking past the front page to less sensational developments of more lasting significance. It wasn't only the news that caught my attention: I also started looking around for investment potential. I don't mean I shopped around in the paper or the business press; I mean I literally looked around in my daily life. I discovered one of my best stocks after I noticed that my kid's friends wore tennies with Velcro closures rather than shoelaces. A secretary I know found a sleeper stock when she noticed that a majority of visiting executives were carrying a certain kind of luggage.

Investment clubs very often take this approach, including my wife's group (profiled in Chapter 10). For the first year, her group tried one hot tip, one broker after another, without much luck. Nothing worked out well, and most of the time they lost money. Finally they said, "Hey, wait a minute. Let's buy into companies that we know something about—the places we shop." So they started buying Nordstrom, Toys 'R' Us, and Safeway. Lo and behold, their investments took off.

In short, everyday events, experiences, even everyday sights take on new significance once you become an investor, or even once you begin to see with an investor's eyes. And that's one of the keys to successful investing: simply paying attention. You don't need any whiz-bang software or rocket-scientist formulas. You need your wits about you. Open your eyes and look around. *What do you see?*

THE BOTTOM LINE
ON INDIVIDUAL STOCKS

- *Buy what you know.*

- *Buy stock only in companies that you'll want to hold on to for years.*

- *Don't invest more than 10% of your total pot in any one stock.*

- *Be cautious about overinvesting in the company you work for.*

- *Get to know the company. Don't bypass research just to get in quick. You have plenty of time to buy a stock that's fundamentally sound.*

- *Throwing money after a hot tip isn't investing; it's gambling, plain and simple.*

- *When you're ready to invest $2,000 in individual stocks, purchase an equal dollar amount of four stocks that look promising.*

- *Don't believe all the hype about new issues; go slow.*

- *You can measure the quality of a stock by its earnings per share (EPS).*

- *The chief yardstick of a company's value is its price/earnings ratio.*

- *Penny stocks are the worst quality stock you can buy, and they have the highest potential for loss.*

- *Impatience is your biggest enemy.*

5

CASH-EQUIVALENT AND FIXED-INCOME INVESTMENTS

Cash-equivalent and fixed-income investments have the most appeal to the conservative at heart. That doesn't mean they're not good investments; it just means that they're more about safety than they are about growth. I'm such a growth enthusiast that, to state it plainly, I would recommend these types of investments only for diversification and liquidity in your portfolio—and only if you're well into your fifties.

That said, a lot of people feel otherwise. It's worthwhile, I think, to understand why.

A WORD ABOUT CAUTION

Many people operate with what seems to me to be an unwarranted or exaggerated sense of caution about the stock market, and a lot of that caution comes from what you could call Depression mentality. The Great Depression of the late 1920s and early 1930s had a profound effect on people, not only those who experienced it firsthand but their kids and even their grandchildren as well. It's left many people skittish about the market; some would sooner put their money in a savings account and let inflation eat it up than invest in stock. Money markets, savings accounts, bonds—somehow, over the years, these types of investments have come to be seen as safe, a concept that, in my opinion, is incorrect.

You have to take an objective look at these so-called risk-free investments, and when you do, you'll find that bonds and cash-equivalent investments, which, to many a man on the street are as safe as it gets, are far from ideal long-term investment solutions. A lot of people are just plain scared, and that fear often sends them straight to bonds, which, I feel, have an undeservedly good reputation. It's my belief that the younger you are, the more you can benefit from stocks, the less you'll benefit from bonds, and the greater the opportunities you'll miss by excessive saving.

If the very idea of bonds and the money market gives you a nice secure feeling inside, step back and examine it for a moment, because you may just be losing out. One drawback to these investments is that cash and bonds don't grow; they only pay interest. And the notion that fixed-income and cash-equivalent investments are risk-free is incorrect, even a myth. Every type of investment is exposed to some kind of risk; the question is what kind and how much. Savings accounts—to some people as safe as it gets—may protect you from the stock market's ups and downs, but they expose you to the very real risk of inflation. And Treasury bonds, another so-called low-risk investment, may be free from default risk, but they are not free from the risks associated with either the market or inflation. So the question isn't which investments are risk-free; the question is what type of risk, and how much of it, can you tolerate?

A MARGIN OF SAFETY

Still, many investors seem to need a margin of safety. And while I feel that need far less than most people and tend to be very aggressive in my investing approach, I'm far from typical. My personal feeling is to consider these types of investments for only two reasons: first, if you need current income from your investments; and second, if you're very close to retirement, because at that point your time horizon for making up any market loss may be shorter. Your temperament may require that you consider otherwise.

An ideal portfolio contains a mix of investments in a sort of three-part harmony: It provides the *return* you need for the *goals* you're pursuing at the level of *risk* you can tolerate. Every investor has different needs and a different temperament, and what works for one won't always work for another. So if fixed-income or cash-equivalent investments seem good to you, they may be, at least for now. And at least you're doing something. But remember to continue investing for growth through other investments. And as always, stick with quality.

CASH-EQUIVALENT INVESTMENTS

Cash-equivalent investments are those that give you easy access to your money, either because they're easily converted to cash or because they have less than one year to maturity. These investments include money market funds, Treasury bills, and short-term certificates of deposit (CDs). Cash equivalents are good investments if you think you might have a sudden need for your money, or if you know you'll need it relatively soon.

In contrast to stocks and bonds, diversification is not especially worthwhile when it comes to these savings-type investments. They all minimize market risk and default risk. Conversely, they all expose you to interest rate risk and a degree of inflation risk. Diversification can't fix that.

MONEY MARKET MUTUAL FUNDS

This is the cash-equivalent investment that I prefer. Money market mutual funds invest in short-term obligations from corporations and from state or federal governments. With these funds it's usually easy to make deposits or withdrawals, and the rates of return fluctuate daily. People often use them as "parking places" for cash in between other longer-term investments. When you are choosing a money market fund, compare your own needs to the fund's particular objective, like tax advantages or potentially high money market returns. Choose a fund from a substantial company. Be cautious about basing your decision solely on highest yield; it may entail too much risk for what should be a low-risk investment.

Money market funds are available from brokerage firms and mutual fund families. Those from mutual fund families offer switch privileges with other funds in the family. Holding a money market fund with your broker enables you to use your account balance to pay for securities.

Investments in money market funds are neither insured nor guaranteed by the U.S. government, and while they are managed to maintain a stable one-dollar share price, there's no assurance that they will be able to. But the flexibility and current income that money market funds can provide make them a good investment. The sweep feature that many such funds have will give you even greater flexibility and liquidity, since it makes your cash available to settle your other trades automatically, without your giving a specific order to sell your money market fund shares. They are also a good savings-type investment. Municipal money market funds invest in short-term obligations from state and local governments, and the interest they pay is not taxed by the federal government, which is great for investors in higher tax brackets. Another type of fund invests exclusively in Treasury bills and short-term agency securities for maximum safety against default. Some Treasury-only funds pay interest that is exempt from state and local income taxes. A global money market fund invests in securities of foreign corporations, banks, and governments; it's often an excellent way to increase yields when U.S. interest rates fall.

All three types of money market funds have five features in common that make them good for *saving*—not investing.

1. You can open a money market fund for little money, usually $500 to $1,000, and make subsequent investments in equally modest amounts (usually $100 or less).

2. Money market funds are managed to minimize risk and default risk, and their securities are restricted to investment-grade quality.

3. Money market funds are immediately liquid, often through check-writing privileges and a debit card. You can convert them to cash without delay or loss of value, which is important when you're depending on them for emergencies and sudden expenses. (CDs, on the other hand, often have withdrawal penalties.)

4. Money market funds generate market-level returns and continually compound the income they pay.

5. All money funds are no-load. They impose an annual fee to pay the manager and cover other expenses, which, while nominal, can vary widely from fund to fund.

TREASURY BILLS

Treasury bills, sometimes called T-bills, are short-term, highly liquid investments available in maturities from three months to one year. They are sold at a discount and return their full face value at maturity. The interest you earn is the difference between the face value of the bill (minimum $10,000) and the purchase price.

T-bills pay market-level interest that is exempt from state tax. The chief problem with T-bills, apart from their high minimum investment, is their inconvenience. You've got to phone a broker or mail paperwork to the Federal Reserve in order to buy them, and you need a broker to sell them. Also, if you need a little money, you can't sell part of a T-bill, and they don't compound indefinitely like money market funds. But they are backed by the full faith and credit of the U.S. government, which is not the case with the other cash-equivalent choices. You can buy previously issued Treasury notes and bonds through brokerage firms and some banks. The advantage is that you get a wide choice of maturities and interest rates, and you can buy at any time, instead of exclusively at scheduled auctions.

CERTIFICATES OF DEPOSIT (CDS)

CDs are issued by banks and savings and loans, pay interest, and return your principal investment at maturity. They are short- and intermediate-term investments, with maturities of three months to five years. The most popular CDs have maturities of three and six months.

CDs have many apparently attractive features—they're guaranteed against default, they pay predictably, and there are no commissions. But it's my feeling that too many investors flock to them without considering other income securities. I'd consider other alternatives for several reasons. For one, CDs from your bank or S&L offer only limited maturities, while bonds offer a range. CDs are not typically liquid, if you cash them before they mature, the bank usually requires you to forfeit interest. Also, interest on CDs is fully taxable; interest on Treasury bills and municipal bonds is not. CDs lock in a rate, which is a disadvantage in a rising-interest-rate environment. Money market funds allow you to keep up with rising interest rates. So in my mind it's a far better idea to put your savings in money market funds, which produce competitive income (in the form of dividends instead of interest) and can be easily converted into cash.

BONDS AND OTHER FIXED-INCOME INVESTMENTS

The key words that apply to bonds and other fixed-income investments are *relative safety* and *regular income.* In terms of protecting your money, these investments are relatively low risk (meaning that it's more than likely that over time you'll end up with the same dollar amount you started with), and they produce regular income. So they're most attractive to three kinds of investors: those who are conservative at heart; those who are close to retirement; and those who have specific income needs.

There are three reasons to consider bonds. First, if safety, rather than growth, is your top priority. This is the most obvious attraction of bonds: the certainty of getting your money back (at its face value) at maturity. Second, if you'll need the money at a specific time, perhaps relatively soon. While I believe that, based on historical performance, stocks will produce your greatest eventual payoff, they don't promise sure and certain returns on a schedule. Third, if you need additional income; for example, if you're retired. For those in a high tax bracket, there are some tax advantages with some bonds. And, of course, many people look to bonds as a means of diversifying their portfolio.

Apart from these situations, I have to say that I'm not a bond enthusiast. If you feel that bonds are a good choice for your portfolio, I'd encourage you to look at high-quality bond mutual funds rather than individual bonds. Beyond that, the world of individual bonds is complex and varied, and you'll need to do some additional research.

A FEW FIXED-INCOME BASICS

Fixed-income investments give you a steady income. The most common fixed-income investments are bonds, which are simply IOUs issued to the investor. The issuer of the bond—the borrower—can be the federal government, a state or local government, or a corporation. The bond states that you have loaned money to the borrower and that the borrower will repay you the full face amount (the amount borrowed) on a certain date, called the maturity date, at a certain rate of interest. The borrower promises to repay you even if the market value of the bond fluctuates over time. Interest is typically paid semiannually, but it can also be paid in a lump sum at maturity. The period of the loan can range from two to thirty years.

OVERSAVING

Apart from not saving at all, the most critical savings mistake people make is to oversave. We've all known someone who has most of his or her net worth in a savings account. Or maybe you know someone who owns several nearly identical savings accounts earmarked for specific goals like kids' college and retirement.

These people know how to save. They just haven't taken the next step: to invest.

The problem is that these savers are using savings vehicles for investing. The purpose of savings is to build an appropriate emergency reserve. Therefore, savings-type investments have to do only two things: preserve capital and keep abreast of inflation. Anyone who tries to meet another investment agenda—growth or income—by using savings-type investments is oversaving.

What's an appropriate level of savings? A lot of people are comfortable holding 10 to 25 percent of their portfolio in savings-type investments. As an alternative, I suggest that you consider limiting this to a sum equaling two or three months of your expenses, which should be sufficient to cover any sudden needs. Money beyond that should be invested in something that can grow over time.

The important point is to consider your savings in the total context of your financial situation. If you have access to reasonably priced credit, like a home equity loan or securities you can borrow against, you don't need to sock away as much money in savings-type investments, where it earns a low interest rate.

This *sounds* like a good deal, and in some ways it is. If safety is your top priority, a bond can be a good investment choice. Conservative types won't lose sleep: the risk of losing your principal, the original amount you invested, is relatively low, or even negligible (excluding junk bonds); and you even make some interest off of it. If the market drops a little, you won't panic.

The problem is that you don't come out much ahead, either, because of inflation. Say you buy a bond for $5,000 with a ten-year maturity. You get interest twice a year, and you know your money's safe. At the end of that ten years, you get your $5,000 back. But not only hasn't it grown, the way it might have if you'd invested in stock, but thanks to inflation it's actually shrunk a little—by 3% a year, or whatever inflation is just then. The money looks the same—the figure has the same number of zeroes, the same 5—but it doesn't have the same purchasing power that it did when you bought it. And while the interest helps, it probably won't do much more than cover inflation. The most powerful feature of a government bond or AAA-rated bond is that you will get your money back (your principal) at maturity (two or three years away). But does this assurance outweigh the risks of inflation and taxes? I think not.

BOND MUTUAL FUNDS

Bond mutual funds give you professional management, liquidity, and a potentially steady stream of monthly income. You can purchase shares through a brokerage firm (some funds are offered only through brokers) or, often, directly from the fund itself. Bond funds are operated by investment companies and are managed by professional investment advisers. They pool money from many individual investors to purchase a variety of bonds and money market securities. As a fund shareholder, you have an interest in every security that the fund holds.

With bonds, especially with U.S. Treasury bonds of intermediate maturity, fund managers have fewer options for adding value than they do with stocks. As a result, the low level of fees within bond index funds (about a quarter of those for broad-based mutual funds) are more likely to have an impact on performance. Statistics have shown that over the last eight years, mutual funds linked to bond indexes have outperformed most of the comparable nonindexed funds.

Bond funds are classified by the types of securities they purchase, such as U.S. government, corporate, or municipal bond funds. Bond funds differ from individual bonds in several ways; for one, they have no maturity date. A bond fund does not necessarily return your principal investment at a predetermined future date. Bond fund shares are not guaranteed; they will fluctuate with market conditions and interest rates, which results in a greater risk to principal with bond funds than with individual bonds. When you want to access your money, you must sell shares in the fund at the current share price—which may be higher or lower than the price you paid for them.

You can choose a fund whose bonds have an average maturity of five years, but since the fund manager will be constantly buying and selling bonds in the fund to maintain that five-year average, the value of your fund shares—as with all bond investments—will vary with changes in market interest rates. You can moderate your interest rate risk by selecting funds judiciously. Funds investing in bonds with shorter average maturities will be less affected by interest rate changes than funds investing in longer-term bonds.

Like all mutual funds, bond funds carry significant tax implications. In most cases, mutual fund earnings are taxed according to the kinds of securities in the fund's portfolio. For example, earnings on corporate bond funds are subject to the same federal, state, and other taxes as earnings from individual corporate bonds. When you sell your fund shares, your tax will depend on the share price at the time of the sale. If the share price is higher than your original purchase price, you'll usually be taxed on the capital gain (the difference between your original cost and the sale price). If the share price is lower, you may be able to deduct your loss from your taxable income.

THE BOTTOM LINE ON FIXED-INCOME AND CASH-EQUIVALENT INVESTMENTS

- *If the idea of investing in bonds and the money market gives you a nice secure feeling inside, step back and examine it for a moment, because you may be losing out.*
- *Cash and bonds don't grow; they only pay interest.*
- *Diversifying savings-type investments is usually not worthwhile.*
- *Money market mutual funds are the cash-equivalent investment I prefer.*
- *If you are drawn to municipal bonds, consider a mutual fund that specializes in tax-exempt bonds.*
- *I believe that bond mutual funds are the best way to invest in bonds.*
- *It's wise to limit long-term bond maturities to five years.*
- *Don't sacrifice quality. Investing in lower-rated junk bonds for a higher yield is a mistake that comes with a huge amount of market risk and volatility.*
- *The purpose of savings is to build an emergency reserve. If you're trying to meet another investment agenda—growth or income—through savings-type investments, you're oversaving.*

6

THE TAXING SIDE
OF INVESTING

Taxes. A lot of people want to bury their head in the sand at the mere mention of the word. But don't give up. Understanding the basics of how taxes affect your investing plan just isn't that hard. You don't have to master the state and federal tax codes, or be a CPA. But it is important. Ignoring the tax implications of investing can cost you a lot of money, and since taxes are the single largest drag on your return, the less money you pay in taxes, the more you will have to invest. Fortunately, this is an area where a little information goes a long way. (That said, remember that these are only the basics. As always, you should consult your tax professional to review your particular situation.)

GENERAL GUIDELINES

We start with some simple guidelines about taxes.

As investors, there are two sides to us:
the tax-deferred side and the currently taxable side.

Think of yourself as two investors. On one hand, you're planning for your future by investing in a government-sanctioned retirement plan—an IRA, a SEP-IRA, a 401(k), a 403(b), a Keogh, whatever is available to you. This aspect of investing should be at the heart of anyone's investing strategy. These plans are a great deal, because the money you invest in them is tax-deferred, meaning that it isn't taxed until you begin to withdraw it (which you can't do without penalty until you're at least 59^1/$_2$). For most of us, taxes will decrease once we retire because we'll be earning less, so that money will be taxed at a lower rate. Meanwhile, during your twenties, thirties, forties, and fifties—potentially four decades, if you're lucky, smart, or both—the whole amount you invest is compounding, free of taxation. That chunk that would otherwise go to the government (30% to 50%) is instead right there working for you, compounding over all those years. Over time, this makes a big difference.

Then there's the currently taxable side, the part of you that's investing outside the tax-deferred accounts. This side of you invests money beyond what you contribute to your retirement accounts (hopefully the maximum) and what you've earmarked for shorter-term goals. When these investments produce income—interest, dividends, or capital gains—you're required to pay current federal and state taxes on that income now (unless you do some planning ahead).

What this means is that some types of investments are better suited to tax-deferred retirement accounts, and others to investing in taxable accounts. So when you look at an investment, you have to decide whether it's going to a tax-deferred account or a taxable account.

Taxes are a great reason to buy and hold in your taxable accounts.

This is a pretty obvious but often overlooked point: By not selling your investments in your taxable accounts, you save money simply because you don't pay taxes on capital gains. Just buy and hold, and by doing so, you can keep the money that would otherwise go to taxes.

Buying and holding is also good advice when you're rebalancing. *Rebalancing* (which is discussed in Chapter 8) means bringing your asset allocation back to its original percentages if, over time, it moves away from those percentages. But if one investment class is lower than you want it to be, you don't have to sell off investments from other classes to bring your portfolio back to your target allocations. If you do, you risk a capital gains distribution—and that means taxes. Instead of selling off the classes over their allocation, you can buy more of the asset class that's low, or you can redirect your dividend reinvestments to it.

Index funds are a good choice for both tax-deferred and taxable investing.

Index funds have a sort of double personality, in that they're a good choice for tax-deferred as well as taxable investing. Sometimes you'll hear somebody say that you shouldn't include index funds in a tax-deferred account because they produce lower realized gains, meaning that you're overdoing it on tax protection. I disagree. I buy the Schwab 1000 Index Fund for both my tax-deferred and my taxable accounts because it provides overall tax effectiveness, lower management fees, and lower turnover costs, which lead to better compounding effects and the most consistent returns. Index funds can be a good choice for the taxable portion of your investments for the simple reason that they minimize capital gains. Since they are geared to match an index, they have a more stable portfolio and see far less turnover than managed funds—and that means fewer distributions. That's what makes them tax-efficient, and a good choice for a currently taxable account.

Pretax return is relevant for tax-deferred investments; after-tax return is what's important for taxable investments, particularly mutual funds.

This is particularly important for mutual funds in taxable accounts, where it's your after-tax return that's important; that's the money you keep. It can appear that a lot of mutual funds are managed as though taxes don't matter—and that may be true, since the managers' compensation is often based on pretax return. For many investors, the biggest problem with mutual funds is the tax implications. The returns from many mutual funds are lower than they seem at first glance, because the taxes the investor has to pay on the dividends and capital gains those funds produce take a big bite out of the return. Most published returns are pretax returns.

If you're investing in a mutual fund in a taxable account, taxes can have a significant effect on your return. In a study conducted at Stanford University, John Shoven and Joel Dickson found that taxes have a significant effect on mutual fund performance. Their conclusion was that "while it is not surprising that taxes lower the accumulations that one can achieve with mutual fund investments over all holding periods, our calculations show that the relative rankings of funds on a post-tax basis (and on our liquidation basis) differ quite dramatically from the published pre-tax rankings. That is, taxable investors cannot easily and reliably determine which of two funds would have offered them a better after-tax return with the publicly-available information."

What's an investor to do? First, be wary of published returns, unless they are the rare after-tax returns. Second, be careful and thorough when you research actively managed mutual funds. Morningstar is a big help here, as they provide a tax analysis for mutual funds.

You should also look closely at a mutual fund's turnover. (Turnover measures how much trading a fund does.) Generally speaking, a low turnover means lower capital gains and lower taxes. Conversely, a high turnover means higher capital gains and higher taxes. It could also mean that the mutual fund manager is incurring tremendous trading costs and tax consequences. Roughly speaking, you should look for a turnover of 100% or less. You can get turnover figures from Morningstar, whose contact information is listed in the Appendix and on the Schwab Web site.

Tax-managed mutual funds are designed to be tax-efficient and are therefore a good choice for taxable accounts.

Tax-managed mutual funds are a small but growing niche; perhaps a dozen or so are available as of this writing. These funds are designed to keep an eye on taxes, and they use several strategies to minimize the drag of taxes on their shareholders' return. They minimize the taxable income they pay in the form of dividends and capital gains, by buying low-yielding stocks or municipal bonds; they reduce turnover; and they offset realized capital gains with losses. And while it's difficult to judge the success of these types of funds because they're so new, it seems that they're off to a good start. In November 1996, *The New York Times* reported that "nearly all of them [tax-managed funds] have accomplished what they set out to do: augmenting their returns by keeping a close eye on taxes." While these funds share common goals, the funds themselves are diverse, ranging from index funds to actively managed stock funds to a mix of stocks and bonds.

Don't invest in securities that produce tax-free income unless you're in a high enough tax bracket to justify it.

Tax-free securities always yield less return than equivalent taxable ones. So you have to be in a high enough federal tax bracket to benefit from tax-free investments. How high is high enough? If you're in a 31% or higher tax bracket, you're smart to consider tax-free income if the net yield (adjusted for tax savings) matches or exceeds that of a fully taxable investment. If your federal tax bracket is 15%, investments that produce taxable income are probably fine for you. You may end up with less return if you purchase investments that produce tax-free income.

Don't be caught off-guard by year-end capital gains with actively managed mutual funds in your currently taxable accounts.

Simply put, this rule often translates to "don't buy actively managed mutual funds at the end of the year," the reason being that mutual funds typically distribute capital gains in December. If you buy shares in a fund in October or November (in a currently taxable account), you'll have to pay taxes on a capital gain from an investment that you've owned for only a couple of months. So you need to plan ahead. You can, on the other hand, invest in index funds in December, because their realized capital gains are low or nonexistent.

The tax consequences of selling shares in a mutual fund can be substantial.

When you sell shares of a mutual fund at a higher price than your original purchase price, you recognize capital gains. Profits on shares that you held for one year or less are short-term capital gains and are taxed at the same rate as ordinary income. Profits recognized on shares that you held for more than one year but not more than 18 months are taxed at a maximum rate of 28%. Finally, profits recognized on shares that you held for more than 18 months are taxed at either 10% or 20%, depending on your income level.

Be aware of the complex record-keeping necessary if you sell a mutual fund.

When you sell shares of a mutual fund, you have to figure out the true cost basis for tax purposes. That is, you have to add to your original purchase price all the dividends and all the capital gains that you reinvested. Doing it yourself is a record-keeping hassle. But the good news is that your broker or mutual fund company should provide you with the average cost per share at year-end.

Generally speaking, all dividend and capital gains distributions produced by a mutual fund are taxable as income. The exceptions are dividends from municipal bond funds or municipal money market funds, which are usually exempt from federal income tax and sometimes from state and local income taxes as well (depending on the tax laws of your state). Each year your mutual fund company notifies you of your total distributions on IRS form 1099-DIV. This form reports all dividend and capital gains distributions you received from your fund holdings. You must report this income on your federal income tax return. It should be presented to your tax professional.

TAX SPECIFICS FOR INDIVIDUAL RETIREMENT ACCOUNTS (IRAS)

Contributing regularly to an IRA is, in many ways, long-term investing at its best. I'd even go so far as to say that for a lot of people, most of their investing dollars should be in retirement accounts. I urge you to make contributions to your IRA (or other retirement account) central to your investing strategy. Here are some general guidelines.

GENERAL GUIDELINES FOR INVESTING IN IRAS

For retirement accounts, don't make tax efficiency a priority in choosing investments.

Suppose you're walking downtown, and it starts to rain. You run for cover and find it in a hotel lobby. All's well, you're warm and dry. Then you notice a guy walking around with an umbrella, inside, still worrying about the rain.

That's what choosing a tax-free investment for a tax-deferred retirement account is like: coming in from the rain and standing under your umbrella. The whole point of investing in retirement accounts is their tax advantages; as soon as you invest in one, you're out of the rain. To choose an investment for the retirement account based on its tax efficiency is redundant; you're doubling up, protecting yourself against something that's already taken care of. You'll be *paying* for it as well, because tax-free securities yield less than equivalent taxable ones. Specifically, tax-free bonds and annuities are not good investment choices for retirement accounts. They're redundant and costly.

Whenever possible, contribute to your IRA early in the year.

The reason is compounding. Making your annual IRA contribution on January 2 rather than waiting until the April 15 deadline of the following year gives your IRA contribution more than 15 "extra" months to grow and compound. This is a time where planning ahead can really pay off. Maybe a salary increase or a bonus can give you an opportunity to make an early contribution to your IRA, or one you hadn't planned on making.

Don't include fixed-income funds in your **IRA.**

It's my feeling that no-load mutual funds are just about the best investment you can make in an IRA. Many investors prefer high-dividend individual stocks to make fuller use of tax deferral. Whatever your preference, don't do what all too many investors do, which is to go for fixed-income funds.

Continue adding to your **IRA** even if you don't qualify for full tax deductions.

The tax deduction of an IRA is only part of the tax-saving benefits. As you put more money into your IRA year after year, the income will continue to grow and compound tax free.

CASE IN POINT: HOW I'VE INVESTED IN MY IRA

In 1982, I decided to check firsthand the value of regular mutual fund investing. I especially wanted to see what I could do using information that's easily available in popular magazines and guides. I wanted to keep it simple, and I decided to test my approach using mutual funds in my Individual Retirement Account (IRA) because tax-deferral of income and capital gains makes tracking returns straightforward.

I set up my IRA at the end of 1982 by contributing $2,000 into a money market fund. Money market funds were paying relatively high rates of interest at the time, and my next two contributions went there as well. That was a mistake. By being on the sidelines in the money fund, I missed a 50% advance in stocks over the next twelve months. Of course, mistakes like that can be rationalized. I had other things on my mind, like selling my company to Bank of America, a deal that was consummated in January 1983. Being preoccupied, I got sidetracked, and it wasn't until early 1984 that I again focused on my IRA. By then I had made three contributions totaling $6,000.

I wanted to select from mutual funds that reflected my philosophy of trying to ride along with the generally upward movement of the American economy. Therefore, I wanted funds that concentrated on companies with accelerating earnings that paid few dividends. Those preferences narrowed my focus to growth funds, small company funds, and international funds. And I wanted good track records.

I found about 50 no-load funds that met those criteria. Then I looked at funds that had stayed in the top-performing 20% for the previous five years, three years, and one year. When I culled the number down to about 10, I compared how they had performed in down markets. I finally selected three growth funds for my IRA. The process took about a half an hour, using performance data available in many publications.

In subsequent years, I put my contributions into additional growth funds, following a similar evaluation technique each time. Along the way, I bought and sold an international fund and added aggressive growth funds and small company funds. Generally I deleted a fund when its performance fell into the bottom half of all funds in its category. It's been my experience that once a growth fund's performance descends to the bottom half, it rarely returns to above-average performance again. So when that happens, it's wise to switch to a better-performing fund. This upgrading approach will keep you from languishing in underperforming funds.

As of this writing, my IRA is made up of 100% stocks, in the form of 14 mutual funds, broken down as follows:

67% in large company stocks in 8 mutual funds

19% in small company stocks in 3 mutual funds

14% in international stocks in 3 mutual funds

How has it done? Pretty well. Even though I've made a couple of mistakes. In 1988 I sold a fund that went up 27% in 1989, and I held on to a fund that experienced below-average returns for an extended time. But from 1983 to 1996, my average annualized return has been 14.9%. If I'd been solely invested in the S&P 500 Index Fund for that entire time, my return would have been 16.5%. I was trying to beat the market and didn't. But my return outpaced inflation by an average of 11.4% per year, which is particularly heartening when you consider that T-bills beat inflation by only 3.3%. And while my contributions to my IRA total only $28,000, its current value is over $118,446. The reason? Compound growth. And *that's* why I urge you to faithfully invest the maximum amount allowed in an IRA.

THE BOTTOM LINE ON TAXES AND INVESTMENTS

- *Pay attention to the tax implications of investing. Taxes are the single largest drag on your total return.*

- *Buying and holding in your taxable accounts can help to minimize taxes.*

- *Index funds are a good choice for both kinds of investing, tax-deferred and taxable.*

- *Tax-efficient mutual funds are a good choice for taxable accounts.*

- *Don't invest in tax-exempt securities unless you're in a high enough tax bracket to justify it.*

- *Anticipate year-end capital gains from actively managed mutual funds.*

III

PUTTING YOUR PLAN INTO ACTION

7

MAKING YOUR INITIAL INVESTMENT

The next step is to actually begin to invest your money. Sometimes people feel nervous about taking the first steps—opening a brokerage account and executing an actual order. But it's not difficult. It's just a matter of doing it.

The process of investing is really just a matter of getting more and more specific. In Chapter 2, you did something very general: you chose an asset allocation plan, a plan for dividing your investment money among the three major types of investments. In Part II, you got more specific: You learned about the advantages of each of those types of investments, and hopefully you got a clearer picture of which ones might best help you meet your goals. And now you'll get more specific still: You'll come up with an investment plan, or a shopping list of specific investments. Which mutual funds? Which individual stocks? Which bonds? Or maybe you'll take the more streamlined approach of using an asset allocation fund. And finally you'll put your plan into action by opening an account with a brokerage firm, purchasing those investments, and beginning to build your portfolio.

1. TURN YOUR PIE CHART INTO AN INVESTMENT PLAN

The first step is to turn the pie chart you chose in Chapter 2 into an investment plan. For example, say you want to end up with 95% of your portfolio in stocks. How much of that 95% should be in large company stocks? How much in small company stocks? How much in international stocks?

What follows are those pie charts again, this time with my suggestions for implementing them.

AGGRESSIVE

If you want your asset allocation to be aggressive, I'd suggest you set up your portfolio this way:

5% money market funds

95% stock mutual funds
40% broad-based U.S. index funds
25% small company index funds*
30% international index funds

0% bond mutual funds

MODERATELY AGGRESSIVE

If you want your asset allocation to be moderately aggressive, I'd suggest you set up your portfolio this way:

5% money market funds

80% stock mutual funds
35% broad-based U.S index funds
20% small company index funds*
25% international index funds

15% bond mutual funds

* If you have the time and interest, this is where you may prefer to substitute actively managed small company mutual funds for further diversification or to try to beat the market. (This is discussed as the "core and explore" approach in Chapter 3.)

MODERATE

If you want your asset allocation to be moderate,
I'd suggest you set up your portfolio this way:

**10% money market funds,
Treasury bills, short-term CDs**

60% stock mutual funds
30% broad-based U.S. index funds
15% small company index funds*
15% international index funds

30% bond mutual funds

MODERATELY CONSERVATIVE

If you want your asset allocation to be moderately conservative,
I'd suggest you set up your portfolio this way:

**15% money market funds,
Treasury bills, short-term CDs**

40% stock mutual funds
20% broad-based U.S. index funds
10% small company index funds*
10% international index funds

45% bond mutual funds

CONSERVATIVE

If you want your asset allocation to be conservative,
I'd suggest you set up your portfolio this way:

**25% money market funds,
Treasury bills, short-term CDs**

20% stock mutual funds
15% broad-based U.S. index funds
5% international index funds

55% bond mutual funds

* If you have the time and interest, this is where you may prefer to substitute actively managed small
company mutual funds for further diversification or to try to beat the market. (This is discussed as the
"core and explore" approach in Chapter 3.)

157

By now, you know I have a bias toward investing a higher portion of each investment dollar in stocks because they are investments that grow. But as a rule of thumb, I believe that if you're over 60, you're probably going to veer toward a more conservative asset allocation, simply because if the market's negative for a few years, it's harder for you to make up your losses. If, on the other hand, you are 45 or younger, I'd suggest you be 95% invested in stocks and stock mutual funds. Still, everyone needs to make the decision based on his or her own comfort level.

2. CHOOSE YOUR INVESTMENTS

Once you have an investment plan, you can get more specific: You decide on specific investments. The worksheet on page 159, "Your Personal Action Plan," will help you to organize what you want to buy.

3. BUILD YOUR PORTFOLIO

Finally it's time to take action: by opening an account. That's very easy to do.

Choose a brokerage firm.

As you consider various brokerage firms, keep in mind that you're not choosing a person; you're choosing a professional firm, the same way you would choose a bank or a real estate company. Don't base your decision solely on a specific broker (even if he or she is a friend or relative); you wouldn't pick a bank because you liked the teller. You'll be doing business with this firm for a long time, so keep factors such as reputation, location, and the breadth of services offered in mind. Now that many people are trading online, reliable technology and a secure system are important considerations as well.

YOUR PERSONAL ACTION PLAN

Investment Category	Investment	Asset Allocation Percentage	Example
Stocks	_____	_____%	Index funds,
	_____	_____%	actively managed
	_____	_____%	mutual funds,
	_____	_____%	individual stocks
	_____	_____%	
	_____	_____%	
Bonds	_____	_____%	Bond mutual
	_____	_____%	funds
	_____	_____%	
	_____	_____%	
	_____	_____%	
	_____	_____%	
Cash	_____	_____%	Money market
Equivalents	_____	_____%	funds, CDs,
	_____	_____%	Treasury bills
	_____	_____%	
	_____	_____%	
	_____	_____%	

Open an account.

Once you've chosen the brokerage firm you want to work with, you simply open an account. It's not all that different from opening a bank account. You'll need to provide personal information such as your Social Security number, and many firms require a minimum starting balance. But once you've opened the account and made your initial investment, you'll be able to buy and sell stocks, mutual funds, and bonds, all from that one account. (There are several types of brokerage or mutual fund accounts; see the Glossary for more information.) To contact a discount brokerage firm, all you have to do is one of the following:

1. Call the brokerage firm on the phone.

2. Go into the brokerage firm's office.

3. Contact them online.

Investing online is a great way to invest; later in this chapter we'll discuss it further. When you make your first contact online, all you have to do is request brochures describing the firm's various brokerage accounts, along with the appropriate application forms. That's it. Then you wait for the literature to come, look it over, and send in your application to get yourself on the brokerage firm's records. Or you may be able to download an application from the firm's Web site. Once you've opened an account, you should be able to trade securities as well as research them online, and you should be able to do it 24 hours a day. Some brokerages offer a discount (10%, for example) when you trade online.

■ ■ ■ ■ ■ ■ ■ ■ ■ ■ ■ ■ ■ ■ ■ ■ ■ ■ ■

IF YOU'RE LUCKY ENOUGH TO HAVE A LUMP SUM

A lump sum is a large amount of cash, usually a onetime payout, that you might receive from an inheritance or in the property settlement from a divorce or the sale of a house, or as retirement income. Whatever the source, receiving a lump sum is both an opportunity and a challenge. It's an opportunity because it can open doors, or at least give you an idea of where the key is. And it's a challenge because you may feel a lot of pressure to do the right thing with that money. "Here's your chance," you think. "Don't make a mistake!"

Well, of course you don't want to make a mistake, but it's wise to try to lessen that pressure. People deal with lump sum distributions in a tremendous variety of ways, and this is most definitely a time to consult your tax adviser and perhaps a financial adviser as well. But take your time. What follows are some general considerations:

I. UNDERSTAND THE TAX IMPLICATIONS.

As always, examine the tax implications carefully. In very general terms, money received as a property settlement in the course of a divorce settlement is not taxable. Money received in an inheritance is the net or after-tax amount, meaning that it's already been taxed, and you keep what you receive. Money received from a retirement plan is taxable, which is why many people opt to open an IRA rollover account, where the money is not taxed until you take the distributions as income. (Another alternative is to receive retirement income in the form of an annuity, meaning that you receive a set amount, which is calculated based on life expectancy tables, each month for the rest of your life.) Capital gains distributions are taxed as well, though at a slightly lower rate than income tax.

2. WHILE YOU'RE CONSIDERING YOUR NEXT MOVE, PUT THE MONEY TO WORK.

As Peter Lynch says, "Money is a great friend, once you send it off to work." And the larger the sum of money, the more work it can do. So while you're considering the best place to invest that money, don't let it languish in a low-interest savings account where, thanks to inflation, its purchasing power will diminish almost daily. Instead, put it somewhere where it can compound a little more—a money market fund is a good "parking place"—while you consider your next move.

3. LOOK CAREFULLY AT HOW INVESTING THIS SUM CHANGES THE BIG PICTURE IN TERMS OF YOUR PORTFOLIO.

How does this sum affect your portfolio? Is it a significant enough amount that you'll want to change your asset allocation? If so, you may want to reexamine your goals and your time frame. Or maybe you'll simply want to "add it to the pot"—in other words, to allocate it in the same way you've allocated the rest of your portfolio, adding a portion to each of your investment classes.

4. TAKE YOUR TIME.

A lot of people, when they receive a lump sum, feel as though they have to act tomorrow, to make an immediate decision about how and where to invest all that money. If you're feeling this way, slow down. The money won't burn a hole in your pocket, or in your bank account. You don't have to decide how to invest it the week after you receive it. You don't even have to decide how to invest the whole thing. Maybe you'll want to invest half of it now by following the same asset allocation you've used for the rest of your portfolio, and think about the rest. You may even take as long as two or three years to decide how to invest it for growth for the long term.

■ ■ ■ ■ ■ ■ ■ ■ ■ ■ ■ ■ ■ ■ ■ ■ ■ ■ ■ ■

Make your initial investment.

So far maybe all this has been a dry run. Maybe you've invested in a specific stock mentally and watched its ups and downs. But that's not enough anymore. As soon as you can, take $1,000—*something*, no matter how little—and actually invest it. You might invest in an index fund that you've watched and researched. If you have a lump sum, you may consider investing it in two or three mutual funds.

Investments other than mutual funds have different requirements concerning the minimum amount of money that you have to have in your account. If you buy a common stock, you'll have three business days to pay for it. For a mutual fund, you have to have your money in your account at the time of the order. Your brokerage firm can describe the specifics for buying and selling different kinds of investments.

Let's say you've decided you want to buy shares in a no-load mutual fund. You'll have to put enough money into your newly opened account to cover the cost of the shares you plan to buy. To do so, you either call, write, or go in personally to the brokerage's branch office. At Schwab, about 5% of our investors come into our office, and another 95% place their orders by computer or phone.

When you place an order, you will need to give the brokerage firm some basic information: your name and account number, the name of the fund (or other investment) you want to buy, and the amount of money you want to invest.

Specify that you want your dividends reinvested.

When you first open your account or when you place your initial order, you'll be asked whether you want your dividends to be reinvested—or in more formal language, how you want to handle "distributions of income." The better choice is almost always to reinvest your dividends and let them make more money for you, before you even have the chance to spend it.

When a company you've invested in makes a profit and pays a dividend, you can look at that dividend in two ways: as income, a nice addition to your checking account; or as a vehicle for growth. Reinvesting your dividends, instead of using them as income, will add fuel to your portfolio growth engine. It's a great way to systematically increase your investment. You can specify that your dividends are to be automatically reinvested in the same stock that generated them, in a sort of vote of confidence; or you can ask that the dividends be put into a separate account to purchase other stocks. Either of these is a productive use of your money. Even better, once you start reinvesting, it's effortless. You don't even have to think about it. And you get rid of the temptation to spend those dividends, in a kind of forced savings. The power of compounding is another very compelling reason to reinvest your dividends.

Choose a money market fund for your cash balances and for short-term investing goals.

Make sure your cash is earning income between long-term investments by signing up for a money market fund or asset allocation fund. This type of fund gives you the potential to earn income on your cash by automatically investing the cash balances held in your account while you are in between other investments. You can choose among money market, U.S. Treasury, government, and tax-exempt funds. These funds are usually designed to offer relative stability of principal, competitive returns, and high liquidity. I recommend that you use a money market mutual fund or an asset management account if you might need the money relatively soon. They're good for short-term investing goals, as a savings vehicle (while you're accumulating enough for an investment requiring a larger minimum), and as a place for emergency funds.

Set up a plan to invest regularly and systematically.

Investing isn't a onetime shot; opening an account and making an initial investment are only the start of a process, not an end in themselves. So give some thought to that process—what *you* want to do to make it as easy as possible to invest regularly and systematically.

There are several ways to set up a system for regular investments. You can authorize a payroll deduction, so that a portion of your paycheck is deducted and automatically transferred to your brokerage account, to be used toward additional investments. Or you can authorize an electronic funds transfer (EFT), in which the money is automatically deducted from your checking or savings account. In either case, the amount of the deduction depends on you. You might start with 5% to 10% of your gross earnings. Or choose a set amount that you think you can afford—$100 a month, or $500 a quarter, for example. Think of it as another item on your budget—it's certainly as important as vacations or entertainment or dining out. Remember that you don't have to stick with the amount you choose initially. Just choose a starting amount, and see how it goes. If, after several months, you find that you can comfortably increase that amount, that's great. As your income increases, you can increase your monthly or quarterly amount.

There are a couple of very good reasons for investing systematically. One of them is something that a lot of us were taught growing up: the idea of a self-tithe, or paying yourself first, meaning that you save some portion of each paycheck or income you receive, and you do it first, before the whole thing gets eaten up.

Another great reason has the complicated-sounding name *dollar cost averaging*. Don't be put off by the name. It simply means investing the same amount of money at regular intervals—for example, $100 a month or $500 a quarter. By regularly investing the same dollar amount, rather than buying a specified number of shares, you automatically buy more shares when the stock price is low, and fewer when the price is up. As a result, you average out the highs and lows of the price. The chart on page 166 illustrates dollar cost averaging.

While dollar cost averaging can't guarantee that your investment will gain or protect you from losses, it can help you buy *more* shares at a lower price, and *fewer* shares at a higher price. It's a natural way to participate in the market throughout its peaks and valleys, and to keep your emotions from short-circuiting your plan. The standard approach is to invest a fixed sum at a fixed interval in one investment. While you can use dollar cost averaging with individual stocks, that involves considerably more risk. The strategy works best on investments that fluctuate in price, such as growth and index mutual funds.

LOWER AVERAGE SHARE PRICE
WITH DOLLAR COST AVERAGING

REGULAR INVESTMENT	SHARE PRICE	SHARES ACQUIRED
$ 400	$ 10	40
$ 400	$ 8	50
$ 400	$ 5	80
$ 400	$ 8	50
$ 400	$ 10	40
Total $2,000	$ 41	260

Average Cost per Share = $7.69
($2,000 ÷ 260 shares)

Average Price per Share = $8.20
($41 ÷ 5)

By regularly funding your account with the same dollar amount, you take advantage of market fluctuations by buying more fund shares when the prices are low, fewer when the prices rise.

Periodic investing (such as dollar cost averaging and dividend reinvestment) requires discipline throughout both rising and falling markets. You should consider your financial ability to stick to this approach. This strategy does not guarantee profit or protect against loss in declining markets. This chart is intended for hypothetical illustrations only, and does not project the future performances of any particular investments.

Check the written confirmation of your order.

When you place an order over the phone, your order will often be executed (meaning completed) during the call itself. If you place your order online, you'll often receive confirmaton very quickly as well. Your brokerage firm will send you written confirmation of your order by mail, usually within three business days. When you receive it, check it to make sure it reflects the information you were given on the phone or online. You should also make sure the transaction is listed on your next account statement from the brokerage firm. Your statement should give a comprehensive picture of the activity in your account during the previous period. It should list all your securities and all your transactions for that period. Make sure the transactions listed are consistent with your other confirmations. I know this sounds tedious, but remember it's your money, and mistakes can happen.

MAKING IT MORE REAL: INVESTING ONLINE

Sometimes investing can seem more like an abstraction than a reality, which is why a lot of people put off doing it. What tangible difference does investing make? You look around your living room, and you see no evidence that you have or haven't done it.

But say you take some action. You open an account, and you set up a system to invest regularly, and it all begins to make sense— except that it can still feel distant. Sometimes when you put money into an IRA or some other kind of retirement account, it can feel like an act of faith, as though that money vaporizes, to return in 20 or 30 years. In the meantime, it's as though that money's locked up tight somewhere far away, in somebody else's care.

Investing online can change that perception dramatically. It's like going from black and white to color. Suddenly investing is *real*— it's all right there in front of you on your computer screen in your office or den or kitchen. And when you can see exactly where your money is and what it's doing, investing becomes as tangible as your living room furniture. You can check the activity of your mutual funds and stocks first thing in the morning or at the end of the day. You can check the prices of investments you're interested in, and you can see what the market is doing as a whole. And you can, of course, track the investments you already own. They're right there in front of you, as real as anything else in the room.

The Internet seems made for investing. It gives you free news, quotes, charts, research, and discounted trading in a timely fashion. If you're already on the Net and are comfortable using it, it's an efficient and cost-effective way to educate yourself, do research, and trade. If you just haven't gotten around to using a computer or the Net much, investing is a great reason to get started.

Suppose you want performance information on the mutual funds offered by your company's 401(k) plan. The Net's informational access and sorting capabilities are perfect for the job. If you're looking for a place to start, Schwab's Web site (*www.schwab.com*) is a good choice.

Once you've opened an account with a brokerage firm, you can use the Net for trading as well as research. After you log on with your account number and password, you can check your investments. You can create a watch list of the investments you own, and maybe some other stocks or funds that you're watching as well. Then you can easily bring up the list, which summarizes the value of your holdings. You can customize how you look at your portfolio. For example, you can have a message alert show up on your screen to alert you when there's a news flash on one of your investments. And you can integrate information from many different sources into one place; for example, if you have accounts with several different brokerage firms or mutual fund families, you can potentially put all that information at one site. In about three minutes, you can see how all your investments are doing.

For a lot of people, going online makes investing more real. And when it becomes more real, you become a more dedicated investor. You begin to feel more in control, both of your assets and of your life.

■ ■ ■ ■ ■ ■ ■ ■ ■ ■ ■ ■ ■ ■ ■ ■ ■ ■

CHEAT SHEET

When you place an order over the phone, you'll need to give your account number. You ask for a quote for the investment you want to buy or sell, and the broker will give you the quote, and if the price is acceptable, you're on your way.

This is a summary of the information you'll need to have ready in order to make a transaction over the phone.

FOR STOCKS

Your account number.

The name of the mutual fund or stock you want to buy or sell.

For buying shares in a mutual fund, the dollar amount you want to invest; for selling shares, the number of shares you are selling.

For buying or selling stocks, the number of shares involved, and whether your order is "at the market" or a "limit order." A limit order is an order to buy or sell a security at a specified price or better. A limit order to sell sets a minimum sales price. Most people place market orders, unless the stock is highly volatile.

If a limit order, whether it's a "day order" or a "good-till-canceled" order. A day order is an order that remains valid until executed or canceled by the customer. At the day's market close, if the order has not been executed or canceled by the customer, it is canceled automatically. A "good-till-canceled," or GTC, order is an order that remains valid until executed or canceled by the customer. At Schwab, all GTC orders that are not executed or canceled by the customer will automatically expire 60 days after the date the order is taken. Unlike a day order, a GTC order can be executed over several days.

Whether you want to reinvest your dividends. I recommend reinvestment, as discussed earlier in this chapter.

FOR BONDS

For bonds, you'll need to provide some additional information, which a bond specialist at your brokerage firm can help you with. This information includes:

The type of bond or issuer.

The face amount (cash value at maturity) and average bond transaction size.

The desired maturity. Bond maturity means the lifetime of a bond, concluding when the final payment of that obligation is due.

Whether you want new securities ("at auction") or secondary market securities.

■ ■ ■ ■ ■ ■ ■ ■ ■ ■ ■ ■ ■ ■ ■ ■ ■ ■ ■ ■

BEGINNERS BEWARE!

You're learning how to invest wisely. Now here's a quick list of things to be wary of.

TREASURE CHEST INVESTMENTS

Treasure chest investments are *things*, tangible investments you can hold—gold, silver, diamonds, coins, art, antiques—as opposed to stocks and bonds. In times of inflation, tangibles can rise appreciably, sometimes even wildly, especially gold. But whether it's old masters and modern art at Sotheby's or precious metals or baseball cards, what goes up thanks to inflation or fear can come crashing down, and without much notice or provocation. To put it bluntly, treasure chest investments are rarely, if ever, good long-term investments, for several reasons, including the high cost of storage, insurance, and security. And they don't generate interest or dividends; they simply tie up your money.

This is not to say that you shouldn't collect what you enjoy; I'm an art collector myself. The point is that if you're a collector, make sure you're doing it for pleasure rather than money.

REAL ESTATE

Owning your own home is wonderful, and it's something that most of us hold very dear and worthwhile. I think of it as an investment in lifestyle, and an important one. But I don't place it in the same category as other investments. I didn't buy my home in order to sell it and make a profit; I bought it to live in it, for personal enjoyment. By contrast, I buy investments to have them grow and prosper on the returns.

While a mortgage brings you tax benefits, the possibility of making significant money on your house is unlikely. The same applies to other real estate, such as a vacation home. And while homes tend to hold their value against inflation, they seldom match an investment return. More important, real estate doesn't grow.

Unless you're planning on going into real estate—just about making a career out of it—and getting involved in the development of property, I'd pass on it as an investment strategy. I know its attraction; I've owned a lot of real estate, and I've been an investor in limited partnerships and major complexes for 30 years. While there are success stories now and then, real estate takes a lot of management and time. If putting your whole life into developing real estate—fixing the place up, selling it for a profit, maintaining it with one renter after another—is a prospect that appeals to you, then maybe it's for you. For my money, it's more time and trouble than it's worth. Think of it this way: You'll never get a call from your stockbroker telling you that the basement is flooded and asking you when you'll be by to fix it. It's my feeling that there are lots of better ways to spend my time.

COMMODITIES AND FINANCIAL FUTURES

Sophisticated investors can use financial futures as hedges or in the transfer of risk over short periods of time. But if you're not an experienced investor, think long and hard before dealing in them. For most of us, putting money in these kinds of investments is like taking our chances in Las Vegas, only Las Vegas might be more fun. We're better off avoiding them.

Commodities, or futures, are contracts traded on an exchange that state a future date of delivery or receipt of a certain amount of a particular product. The key word is *future*, and the product may be any one of a variety of things: agricultural, such as wheat or pork bellies; oil; metals; financial instruments. Speculators generally invest in these contracts at a price they hope they can turn into a profit way before the commodity is ever delivered. These are instruments used by professionals for hedging and speculation. The individual who is able to make money in commodities is rare.

OPTIONS: PUTS AND CALLS

A call is an option to purchase a stock at a set price for a set time period. Those who buy calls are betting that the price of the stock will go above the set price, and the difference will be their profit. With puts, it's the reverse. Here the investor is hoping that the stock will drop in price. Most put and call options are traded on the American Stock Exchange in New York, the Chicago Board of Options Exchange, the Philadelphia Stock Exchange, and the Pacific Exchange.

I consider puts and calls a short-term approach to investing, and since I advocate mostly long-term techniques to build up a solid asset base, these strategies, to my mind, have a limited value. In order to make a profit, you have to be right more often than not over periods of just a few months, which is tough to do. In short, I suggest that you wait until you're very comfortable with investing before you try using option strategies.

FULL-COMMISSION BROKERS

As an investor, it's crucial to understand how your broker is compensated. Are his or her earnings derived primarily from commissions (commission-based service)? Or are they derived from salary and advisory fees (fee-based service)? It's an important question because a broker who is paid on a commission basis may try to sway you to put your money in investments that will be lucrative to him or her, rather than in the best possible investments for you. In past years I've noticed that often in the world of full-commission brokers, the riskier the investment, the higher the broker's commission. Some brokers consider these commissions a sales incentive; I call them conflicts of interest. Discount brokers are fee-based brokers, meaning that they are salaried; they do not receive commissions on sales.

The point is that it's crucial to understand your relationship with your broker. To do that, all you have to do is ask how he or she is paid—on salary or on commission. Advice is great, as long as it's coming from someone independent of the transaction, someone who has no monetary interest in what you buy. If you can't spare the few hours a month it takes to manage your investments, or if your financial situation is fairly complex, consider using a fee-based investment manager or financial adviser, an alternative that we'll discuss more fully in Chapter 10.

SHORT SELLING

Short selling is, to a lot of people, very tempting. It's tricky business, involving borrowed stock and relying on an investor's knack for spotting an overvalued stock, something that takes quite a bit of experience to be able to do. Here's how it works. You borrow shares from your stockbroker, then immediately sell them, hoping that everyone else is about to become aware of a flaw in that stock and sell it off, bringing the price down. Once the price has dropped way down, you snap up enough shares to repay the broker, and you keep the difference between the high price at which you sold the shares you'd borrowed from the broker and the low price at which you bought the payback shares.

It sounds like a great plan, but it's more of a scheme, and one that's often doomed. A lot of people focus on the upside of this scenario—its potential rewards—but the downside is pretty serious. If you're wrong about that stock, and it goes up instead of down, you owe the broker for the new cost of those shares. And there's no telling how high those shares can go.

When you own a stock outright, the worst—the very worst—that can possibly happen is that the stock goes to zero, in which case you lose the total amount you invested in that stock. But when you sell short, you can lose all your money. Your potential loss is unlimited, because there's no limit to how high a stock price can go. I can't forget a case in the 1960s, when a friend of mine shorted Xerox, and the stock just kept going up. He lost 300% to 400% of his money and was wiped out.

I have to add that there's nothing intrinsically wrong with short selling. *Barron's* considers it "a legitimate investment technique," and it includes short-sale recommendations in money manager interviews. My caution about short selling can be summed up in three words: *very high risk.* It is definitely an only-for-the-pros endeavor, requiring a great deal of experience, diligence, and attention.

PERMANENT LIFE INSURANCE

Put bluntly, it's my feeling that for many years the life insurance industry has abused a lot of people. It has certainly set up an amazing incentive system for its salesmen, and it seems to be true that the worse a life insurance policy is for the customer, the better it is for the insurance company and the agent. Some companies seem to try to sell insurance based on fear rather than on its real basis: the possibility of premature death.

Permanent life insurance, also called "whole life" insurance, is really a decreasing term life policy with an increasing, low-interest savings account. This means that every year, your life insurance protection decreases as your "cash value" (savings account) increases. But the cash value in that savings account doesn't build up during the first two years, because during that time all the premiums are paid out in commissions to the salespeople.

I think the best thing to do in terms of insurance is to look for a good *term policy*. You'll find more information in the Glossary under "insurance."

* * *

A thousand reasons can keep you out of the market, but I don't think you should let them do it. Every year for the past 30 years, some economic or political turmoil has made it seem intuitively illogical to invest, from the Cuban missile crisis to the S&L bailout and even a raging bull market. But the market has always recovered. Compound growth can't work for you if you don't invest. So I urge you to start investing intelligently—and to stay with it.

THE BOTTOM LINE ON TAKING THE FIRST STEPS

- *Investing is not a onetime shot; opening an account and making an initial investment are only the start of the process.*

- *To get started with an investment program, choose the brokerage firm you want to do business with, open your account, and make your initial investment.*

- *Reinvesting dividends is a great way to systematically increase your investment.*

- *Make sure your cash is earning income between long-term investments by signing up for a money market fund.*

- *Set up a plan to invest regularly and systematically.*

- *The Internet is a great way to educate yourself, do research, and trade.*

8

FOLLOWING UP ON YOUR PLAN

Think of it as an investment checkup. Once or twice a year, you should take a look at your investments and see how you're doing. Does your portfolio still reflect your investment goals? Do the percentages in your brokerage account match up with that pie chart you chose in Chapter 2? A lot of investors find that tax time and year-end are good opportunities for this reexamination.

There are three basic steps to reviewing your investments.

I. REVIEW YOUR ASSET ALLOCATION PLAN

Take another look at your pie chart in Chapter 2. Are you still comfortable with the asset allocation plan you chose? If you are, you'll need to make sure your portfolio still reflects those percentages. But maybe you've changed since you adopted that plan. Investors often do; a little time, a little experience, and all of a sudden you're a lot more comfortable with all of this and not just willing but eager to be a little more aggressive. In my own case, as my knowledge and confidence and experience have grown, I've become more aggressive. Don't be afraid to change your asset allocation plan—to choose a different pie chart—if you're so inclined. And if you find you want to change your plan, bring your portfolio in line with the new percentages you want by rebalancing.

2. IF NECESSARY, REBALANCE YOUR PORTFOLIO

Rebalancing simply means bringing your asset allocation back to its original percentages. Remember that how you allocate your portfolio among different types of investments (stocks, bonds, and cash equivalents) is considered the most significant factor in your rate of return. One of the easiest ways to rebalance is to do it online. It's one of the great uses of technology, and your brokerage firm should offer you this capability.

For example, suppose you chose an asset allocation plan of 60% stocks and 40% bonds. After several years, you find that because stock prices have increased, 70% of your investing dollars are now in stock funds, and only 30% in bond funds. When you chose your original asset allocation, your decision was based on the risk you were willing to accept, and the potential rewards a specific allocation might offer. Given that, it follows that if your stock holdings rise above your original allocation, your exposure to risk increases, just as if your stock holdings fall below that original allocation, your future growth potential is probably lower. So the first question is whether or not you want to return to that 60/40 model. If you do, there are three ways to do it:

1. You can sell the holding that is over the target percentage and reinvest the money in other investments. In this case, you'd sell 10 percent of your stock funds, and use that money to buy bonds.

2. You can increase the total dollar amount you have invested and buy more of the investments that are low, in this case bonds.

3. You can instruct your brokerage firm to direct dividends away from the high investment and into the low one, in this case from stocks to bonds.

If your investments are in a tax-deferred account, taxes are not a concern for now. If they are outside tax-deferred accounts, you'll have to consider the tax implications when rebalancing your portfolio. This is an important time to consult your tax professional, or to study the tax considerations yourself. I'd recommend that you avoid selling investments that have appreciated, because if you sell them, you'll incur capital gains. Methods 2 and 3 are both ways to rebalance without selling and hence without paying capital gains taxes. (Because I'm a long-term investor, I look at my statement with an eye toward change—meaning selling—only once a year. The rest of the time, in the interest of my peace of mind, I don't even consider it.)

3. BENCHMARK: EXAMINE THE PERFORMANCE OF EACH INVESTMENT

It's human nature to want to know how you're doing, so during your investment checkup, take some time to compare how each individual stock and mutual fund you own is doing relative to its respective benchmark. When you do this, remember: *You don't have to beat the index. You just want to be close to matching it.*

Tracking the performance of your investments isn't hard; it's based on common sense as much as anything. Your statement from your brokerage firm should give you all the information you need. Next, consider how your investments are performing relative to the market. My preferences for comparison are the S&P 500 Index and the Schwab 1000 Index. (Some people like the Dow, but I'm less enthusiastic about it. It includes just 30 stocks, and they're all from blue-chip corporations, so it's narrower than other indexes.)

The "Benchmarking Guide" that follows contains my suggestions for the index to use for various types of investments.

Say a mutual fund in your portfolio went up 10% in a given year, and the S&P 500 Index also went up 10%. That's fine, because, as I've said, you don't have to outperform the market to do well.

BENCHMARKING GUIDE

IF YOU OWN:	BENCHMARK AGAINST THIS INDEX:
Individual stocks Balanced funds Growth funds Aggressive growth funds Equity and income funds Index funds Precious metals and gold funds Specialized funds Flexible portfolio funds	S&P 500 Index and/or Schwab 1000 Index
Small company funds	S&P 500 Index and/or Schwab Small Cap Index
Global equity International equity Emerging markets Pacific equity Europe equity	Morgan Stanley EAFE Index
Bond funds	An index from Lehman Brothers that matches the kind of bond fund you have. For example, you would benchmark short/intermediate-term high-quality corporate bonds against the Lehman Brothers Intermediate Term Corporate Bond Index.

Matching the market is absolutely acceptable. If, on the other hand, your fund went down 2%, and the S&P went up 8%, that's a sign that something's gone awry, and you'd better keep an eye out. Watch it for a while longer, and if the trend continues, it might be time to change.

In a downmarket scenario, your growth fund might go down 15% while the S&P 500 is down only 12%. In my mind this is an acceptable relative performance. I'd recommend holding on to the fund. Your fund may be slightly more volatile, but it's in the same ballpark.

Next, compare the performance of your investments against that of their peers. It's important to use the right "peer group." For example, if your fund is an international equity fund, you'll want to evaluate its performance against similar funds.

■ ■ ■ ■ ■ ■ ■ ■ ■ ■ ■ ■ ■ ■ ■ ■ ■ ■ ■

YOUR BIG PICTURE

It's easy to find out the yield of your money market fund, but most people don't know how all of their investments combined have performed—in other words, their total rate of return. A common mistake people make is reading that their mutual fund returned 12% in a given year and being lulled into the idea that their entire portfolio returned 12%. But if only 50% of your money is in the mutual fund, while the other 50% is in the money market fund earning 4%, your total return is only 8%. That's why you may want to figure out the rate of return for the *total amount of money* you have in all your savings and investment accounts.

Here's a useful way to come up with a ballpark figure:

1. Compare your year-end statements from last year to your current one.

2. Subtract any new money you added during the year from your current balance.

3. Take the remainder, and divide it by your balance from the end of last year.

4. If the result is greater than 1, you're ahead. If, for example, your result is 1.12, you're up 12%.

This simple method isn't precise, but it's useful.

Remember that for your taxable accounts, your return is a before-tax figure. If you have a 10.4% before-tax return and you're in the 36% federal and state tax bracket, your after-tax return is really only 6.65%.

A computer spreadsheet is a great tool for calculating rates of return. Your brokerage firm's Web site or your financial adviser may also assist you with obtaining these figures.

■ ■

WHEN TO CONSIDER SELLING YOUR INVESTMENTS

The fact is that our investment decisions don't always turn out to be good ones, and there are certainly times when it's time to cut your losses and sell a specific investment. But you don't sell after only a few weeks or months. Because of the market's emotional nature, its day-to-day or even week-to-week fluctuations usually aren't significant buy-or-sell indicators; they're just movement in that organic entity we call the stock market.

MARKET TIMING

A lot of people think of investing as a constant buy-sell endeavor, and they picture themselves watching the ticker tape and trading like crazy, based on what the market does day to day. The appeal of market timing is seductive: Get in when stocks are headed up, and get out when they head back down. But there are two very compelling reasons for staying in the market—in other words, buying and holding—rather than getting in and out: taxes and market efficiency. The longer you're in the market, the more you're exposed to its rewards. And any losses you do incur are only "on paper" until you sell.

Taxes have a huge effect on those rewards, and they are a very strong argument for not selling. Quite simply, if you don't sell, you don't pay taxes on the sale. And if you don't pay taxes on the sale, that 30% to 35% of the profit money that would otherwise go to the government stays in your portfolio and continues to work for you.

During the 1980s, the S&P 500 compounded at an unusually high 17.5% annually. There were 2,528 trading days in that decade. If you weren't invested during the ten top-performing days of those 2,528, your rate of return would have been 12.6%. If you missed the market's 20 top-performing days, your growth rate would have been only 9.3%. If you missed the market's 30 best days, you'd have earned only 6.5 percent. And if you were on the sidelines during the 40 finest days—40 days out of ten years—your return would have been only 3.9 percent. I know it's unlikely that a person timing the market would sit out only the best days. But the largest gains regularly come when conditions look darkest—and that's when a market-timer is least likely to be invested. So market timing can keep you out of the market at the wrong time. (This is not to say that you can't improve your success by studying market cycles and through hands-on experience.)

Instead of trying to predict the market's ups and downs and then buying and selling accordingly, a good alternative is to be in the market continually. Invest for the long term, and be very picky about when you even *consider* selling. Think about selling only when you want to rebalance your portfolio or change your allocation, or when, after a significant amount of time, an investment's performance isn't satisfactory compared with benchmark results.

When should you buy? A lot of people seem to think there's a perfect time for buying stocks, and they are determined to spot it, and they won't invest until they do. When the market goes up a little, they say, "Now? Invest now? But if I do, I'll buy at the high. I'm scared to death, everything's so high. I better wait until prices come down!" And sure enough, prices do come down temporarily. But do these people invest then? "No way," they say. "I'll wait until it goes down a little more, get a bargain." It does go down a little more, and then they get really scared, figuring the bottom's dropping out, and when it starts back up, they figure they missed it, and that takes care of that.

But here's the thing: There is no magic moment, no perfect time to buy. As it turns out, onetime is almost as good as any other. The important thing is to get in there and do it now. And while someone who invests now might do better or worse than someone who invested six months ago or who will invest six months from now, in the long run the difference turns out to be negligible. Timing is a very minor player in the larger scheme of investing.

WHEN TO SELL MUTUAL FUNDS

Mutual funds are core investments. As such, I don't see selling them very often. In fact, personally, I tend to buy them and hang on to them for a minimum of three years, most of them a lot longer than that. In my experience, three years is a fairly typical cycle, and it usually includes a down market and an up market. I like to see how the managers of a fund perform through the test of a down market.

It's pretty simple: You monitor the fund's performance. If the fund is performing as well as the general market—if it's matching the S&P 500 or the Schwab 1000 Index—you hang on to it and possibly add to it. If and when you think, after a reasonable amount of time, that it isn't performing as well as it should, you can switch to another.

WHEN TO SELL INDIVIDUAL STOCKS

If you've done your homework and bought an individual stock only after a lot of thought, a drop in its price is not, in and of itself, a good reason to sell. The stock may or may not be going downhill. Stock investments are long-term commitments, so a drop in price or a so-so performance over several years may not be reason for worry. If you've chosen a wide variety of individual stocks (or invested in a broadly diversified stock mutual fund), it's likely your investment portfolio will appreciate steadily over time, overcoming most temporary setbacks.

That said, I have to add that if you've made a bad decision and followed a hot tip or bought without researching, there comes a point when it's time to cut your losses and sell. But that's different from letting the natural growth of a company unfold over time.

Keep in mind that most investors are simply too emotional. A little bad news can spread worry and send a stock way down, but only temporarily. A slight economic downturn can also have a temporary negative effect. Say you've invested in a company that's related to the housing market, and interest rates go up. The housing market may go down, but it's probably temporary. Christmas sales are another example. A great stock can take a hit at Christmastime simply because everybody's running to some new gadget, and a tried-and-true, great-performing stock can suffer. But it's a temporary effect, not necessarily a big deal, and often the stock will bounce back up pretty quickly. In the larger scheme of things, the company's competitive position isn't usually significantly affected, and that Christmas downswing often turns out to be just a blip on the screen.

A more serious indicator of trouble than stock price is market share. If a company starts losing its market share, that's a different story. It may be the time to get off that boat. If the company's competitive position is eroding, or if its industry is eroding in what looks like a permanent way, the situation is far more serious. If the stock prices of similar companies are going up and yours is going down, you may have a legitimate cause for concern.

There's plenty of information available to help you track stock performance, and once again, the Internet is probably the best place to start. That's where you'll find the timeliest and most easily accessible information. Many magazines and newspapers publish analysts' reports on investments, economic trends, and developments in different industries. Many quality investment reference books and newsletters also provide professional and objective information. (You'll find listings in the Appendix.)

SURVIVING A DOWN MARKET

In order to climb the stock market's peaks, you have to pass through its valleys. It's tough enough to hold your emotions at bay during the normal downturns, but somewhere in your lifetime, chances are you'll face a formidable down market. Eventually stocks recover to new highs, but many investors lose faith before the recovery and flee to "safety"—cash equivalents and fixed-income investments. As a result, it's virtually impossible for them to catch up when the market does turn around. After a 30%, 40%, or 50% loss, you need a 60%, 80%, or 100% gain to break even. You'll never get it if you've sold your stocks in fear, retrenched, and settled for a loss. As stocks recover in the next upswing, you will watch with disgust, but never return.

So once you adopt a sensible investment plan, I believe you have to commit to that plan and believe in the soundness of its logic. You'll need that belief to sustain you through the inevitable bad times. Logic and good sense alone won't do it, because when the market starts a downward spiral, every logical, sensible voice will be telling you to abandon your plan and run. Only an unshakable belief in yourself and in the long-term future of American enterprise will keep you on course and in the market.

When the market falls to a painful low, you'll start to believe everyone who's saying the country is headed to ruin. When your fears are at their peak, you must make an extra effort to resist them. Tell yourself, "Don't give in." Instead, know that history has shown that American financial markets come back from every apparent abyss. When the market soars to dizzying heights, you'll again be torn by the other emotions of investing. At breakfast you'll decide to mortgage the farm to buy more stocks. At lunch you'll decide to sell everything while it's high. Do neither. Just sit tight.

Down markets are the times that try our souls, all right, because our pocketbooks are involved. But you have to keep the broad picture in mind. During the past 100 years we've had 25 bear markets. Some were worse than others, but the typical bear prowled around for about nine months and took the market down 25 to 30 percent. Every single one of them was followed by a bull market. Every one of those bull markets attained new highs.

Remember that record. It tells me that I'm investing in something that has always come back, and I believe it always will. Maybe you will buy in at the peak. If so, the market will fall as it always has. And it will probably recover, just as it always has. When you truly understand—emotionally and intellectually—that record, you'll see that today's picture means nothing for your life and goals 10 or 20 years from now. That understanding is the foundation upon which you can construct your financial future.

BECOMING A WELL-ROUNDED INVESTOR

Once you buy some shares in a mutual fund, you may soon find yourself opening up the business section of the newspaper each morning to see how it's doing. If you invested a little in a favorite company, a brief news item on the back page, something you wouldn't have noticed a month ago, may now catch your attention. That's because you're becoming involved. It's natural, once you begin investing, to get more and more interested in the world of investing. If you do want to learn more about it, there are plenty of places to look.

But don't overdo it. Take a look at a newsstand, and you'll see what I mean: There's plenty to read in the world of investing. A lot of beginning investors feel like they have to read it all, and they'd better do it by dinner. But you don't. I'm suggesting that you become an informed investor, not an expert. Take it a little at a time, and before long you'll be amazed at how much you know.

The suggestions listed here are enough to get started. Remember, you don't have to follow them all at once. Solid portfolios are not built in a day. Becoming a well-rounded investor doesn't mean heading back to school for an MBA or subscribing to every financial publication available. It just means becoming conversant in the language of investing. You'll find yourself doing some of these things on your own. (You'll find more information in the Appendix.)

1. Read the financial pages of your local newspaper.

Once you start to keep tabs on various stocks and watch their daily quotes, you'll be surprised at how quickly you get interested in figures that didn't used to mean much to you. But keep your emotional distance; just observe, don't react. Remember that the media tend to like the hype. After all, it's the stock market's ups and downs—not its steady performance over time—that makes news.

2. Read the financial section of a national newspaper.

Most investors find that they want to watch the market more closely once they've made their first investment. For Monday-to-Friday reading, I like *The Wall Street Journal,* the nation's best business newspaper. You don't have to read every word, just the highlights. I like to start on page C1. The first pages tell what stock prices did the previous day, with charts that show market trends.

Investor's Business Daily is also good. The financial section of *USA Today* is useful, as are the business pages of *The New York Times, The Los Angeles Times,* and *The Chicago Tribune.* You'll learn to pay attention to what's relevant and skip what's not. You should certainly look at the page-one news summary of events that may have had a temporary effect on the prices of your stocks. The more you are able to connect the events, reports, and fears of the day with stock prices, the more you will understand market cycles.

3. Become familiar with one or more investors' magazines.

It's a good idea to read at least one investors' magazine. There are lots to choose from; I find *Forbes* and *Money* to be the two best and most comprehensive for typical investors, although *Fortune, Business Week, Smart Money,* and *Barron's* are also very good. Their pieces on specific companies are often very informative and insightful. Because so much good material is available, you'd be wise to limit your reading only to what's relevant to your investing strategy. Find the publications that best suit your needs.

4. If necessary, consider an investment advisory service.

I say "consider" because this step is certainly optional. For one thing, the services offered by companies like Value Line and Standard & Poor's can be on the expensive side. But an advisory service can be very helpful in the early, learning stages of investing, and you may find it worth the money. Some good professional services are available; the trick is to shop around. You might start by looking in *Barron's* or *Forbes* for some possibilities. Or maybe you'll hear of a good one by word of mouth. Peruse them in your library or on the Internet, and then, if you're interested, take out a trial subscription.

You're looking for integrity and objectivity. Try to find out about the history of the advisory service you're considering, so that you can examine its track record and determine how effective it is. The services are all different, so this can take a bit of research on your part. But the right one is out there, at a cost-effective price, if you feel you need the help.

THE BOTTOM LINE ON FOLLOWING UP

- *Take a look at your investments once or twice a year to see how you're doing: review your asset allocation plan, decide whether your portfolio needs rebalancing, and examine the performance of each investment.*

- *I'm a strong advocate of buying and holding. There are sound reasons to stay in the market instead of trying to get in and out at the right time.*

- *Taxes have a huge effect on your returns and are a very strong argument for not selling.*

- *Invest for the long term, and be very picky about when you even consider selling.*

- *There is no magic moment to invest.*

- *Mutual funds are core investments. I don't see selling them often.*

- *The best source for timely fund information is the Internet.*

- *Stock investments are long-term commitments.*

- *Once you adopt a sensible investment plan, commit to that plan, and believe in the soundness of its logic. You'll need that belief to sustain you through the inevitable bad times.*

9

BRING THE KIDS

FAMILIES AND INVESTING

Having children, as any parent knows, changes your life dramatically. Not surprisingly, having a family will affect your investment plans as well, influencing everything from how you invest to the tax implications of the investments themselves. And it's important that you educate your children in financial matters as well.

STARTING THEM EARLY

Sad to say, managing personal finances isn't something our kids learn about in school. So we as parents need to take responsibility for our kids' educations in this area. We already do it in other areas; we don't expect the schools to take sole responsibility for our children's moral or religious upbringing. Oddly enough, finances are in the same boat. We need to teach our children to take care of themselves financially, how to do the right thing for their long-term security. By involving the whole family in finance, you'll all understand why you're doing what you're doing where the money is concerned. Don't just invest *for* your kids; invest *with* them. Think of yourselves as a family of investors.

Exposing kids to some of the principles and practicalities of investing at a young age can get them off to a good start. By involving your kids in the investing decisions you make—meaning, at a minimum, informing them—you're doing them a big favor. You're starting them early and increasing their chances of becoming committed investors themselves. You'll find that kids turn out to be great investors. Give them a little cash, and they'll jump at the chance to invest it in something, if you've taught them how and why. It can be a good experience, and while it may be a little frustrating as well, the kids will learn far more by doing than they will in a classroom.

Specifically, I'd encourage you to do the following:

As you're developing your investing strategy—your asset allocation plan—explain the issues and trade-offs involved to your family. Even if you're the one who's really making the decisions, it's important that your spouse and kids understand why you're making them.

Teach your children well. Don't let them think that investing is a onetime act. Let them see that it's an activity by teaching them to read monthly statements. Pick up a *Wall Street Journal* or the business section of your newspaper and show them how to track your investments.

Make it personal. Setting aside a small amount of money to buy stock in a company that means something to your family is a great hands-on lesson for kids. Maybe the company stands for something you believe in—it's environmentally or socially responsible, for example. Maybe you just like what it makes or does, its sneakers or snowboards or software. In any case, it's a company your family is rooting for. Your affection or admiration for that company can make investing more personal. I'm not talking about following a hot tip; I'm talking about following your heart *with a very small percentage of your money.* Another way to make investing personal is to buy a no-load mutual fund in a family member's name, then persuade him or her to monitor its performance on the market pages. And then you can explain diversification.

PASSING IT ON

My father, though he was a lawyer, had a healthy interest in the stock market, and when I was about 13, he gave me my first glimpse at investing. He held out the stock page of the newspaper and said, "These things go up and down."

And I began to watch a couple of them. I'd choose one and ask him to buy some of it for me, and he'd nod and go back to his paper, meaning that I didn't really buy anything—we both understood that my investing was only mental. But it still counted, to me at least.

Often one of those mental investments would go up, and sometimes it would even double or triple in a relatively short time. I found all those ups and downs—all that movement in the market—fascinating from the start, and I began to watch for something I could really buy. I'd saved up about $100 from all those chickens and walnuts and other odd jobs, and I finally settled on a one-dollar stock and bought 100 shares. For a long time after that, I faithfully and enthusiastically watched the market.

Years passed, and eventually I found myself in my father's place, teaching my own sons about the market. They were teenagers when we started, and they both got interested.

My eldest son—16 instead of 13—chose a few stocks, and they went up. I got him more interested by telling him about a couple of companies. Once again, he chose a few, and they went up.

Next I bought him some shares in two high-tech growth companies and told him he could pick a third. He chose Chrysler, even though, at that time, it was heading downhill. His choice wasn't based on any in-depth analysis—he just knew that the name was familiar and that, because the price was low, he could buy a lot of shares. Sound familiar? It may—it's an approach a lot of beginning investors mistakenly adopt, confusing quantity with quality.

So he bought into Chrysler, with $100 he had earned himself. And guess what? He got lucky. Lee Iacocca was in charge, the stock price climbed from $3 to $30, and my son's investment went up ten times. It did much better than the other stocks I'd suggested. And he learned the thrill of investing, something I suppose both he and my youngest son have come by honestly.

■ ■

INVESTING FOR YOUR CHILDREN'S FUTURE

From the time she was in kindergarten, your daughter wanted to be a doctor; from the second your son got the lead in the school play, all he's talked about is doing Shakespeare someday. Or maybe you've always promised yourself you'd help your kids with a down payment on their first home.

Whatever the goal, start by giving some thought to the financial goals you and your children may have, so that you can answer those "how much" and "how soon" questions. But remember, investing for your children's future is no different from investing for your own retirement or for that longed-for traveling. Whatever your goal, the pie charts in Chapter 2 will help you determine your investing plan. What follows here are simply general observations about your possible goals for your children.

College

A year at a public college today costs an average of $9,646 for tuition, books, fees, room and board, and personal expenses. At a private college, the price is about $20,361 a year, according to *The College Board Annual Survey of Colleges, 1996*. And those high costs are for 1996; think what a college education will cost in five, ten, or fifteen years from now. *The Princeton Review Student Access to Paying for College* (1996 edition) estimates that college tuition costs will continue to rise by 5% to 6% per year, well above the current rate of inflation. In just ten years, you could easily be paying $67,722 for a four-year degree at a public college, and up to $142,949 at a private one.

The good news is that you may not have to supply all the money required for college. Millions of today's students receive government loans, grants, and scholarships. Still, in light of the increasing costs, it's crucial to start investing early, while your child is still relatively young.

Graduate or Professional School

Today a bachelor's degree just doesn't go as far as it used to; in a lot of cases, it's not enough to get the hoped-for job or career. So more and more college graduates are pursuing graduate degrees. And an advanced education does, of course, mean advanced tuition and other costs.

A First Home

Today most people in their twenties need financial help from their parents in order to buy a first home, and house prices are expected to continue to go up. According to the National Association of Realtors, the median price of an existing single family house sold in June 1997 was $123,700. Given that the average down payment plus closing costs is around 20%, the first-time home buyer needs a lot of money.

Starting a Business

Maybe you've raised a budding entrepreneur—your daughter wants to open a restaurant, or your son (or grandson) has a great idea for a small business. You want to help him or her get started.

You have plenty of reasons to plan ahead for your kids' financial futures. Luckily, you also have plenty of ways to do it. By starting early, the money you invest for your children's future can match, if not outpace, inflation.

SOME TAX CONSIDERATIONS

The tax considerations for investing for your children are significant, both in terms of income tax and gift tax. Tax laws and regulations are complex and they change frequently. You should consult your tax professional to review the tax consequences of your particular situation. What follows are general guidelines and suggestions.

Income Tax

The Tax Reform Act of 1986 introduced a new set of rules called the "kiddie tax" for children under 14 with investment income. It changed tax rules for each of the three kinds of accounts you might use for a child's funds.

If you hold an account in your own name, even though it's intended for the children's benefit, you get no special tax breaks. The investment income is taxed in the usual way, at your own tax rate.

If you have a *custodial account* for a child under 14, the first $650 (periodically adjusted by an inflation index) of its yearly unearned income (dividends and interest) is free of federal income tax. The second $650 is taxed only at the child's rate, presumably the minimum 15%. Any additional income is taxable to the child but at the parents' top marginal rate—the tax rate you pay on your last dollar of income. One potential investment strategy in this tax situation might be to develop a mixed portfolio with enough high-income-producing securities to generate taxable earnings up to the $1,300 ceiling, with the balance invested in tax-free securities or high-growth, low-dividend stocks. Note that the money or investments in a custodial account will belong to your child when he or she reaches the age you specify when you set up the account. The child may not choose to use it for the purpose you intended. If this is a concern, you may want to opt for an account in your own name.

For children 14 or over, tax rules are more liberal. Their first $650 in yearly unearned income is still free of federal income tax, but all additional earnings are taxed only at the child's rate. A child this age could have unearned income of $23,350 before exceeding the 15% tax bracket. These figures are, of course, subject to change.

With a properly drafted *irrevocable trust*, a different set of tax rules apply. You'll need the advice of an attorney to prepare the trust documents. You should also consult a tax adviser to prepare your tax returns.

Gift Tax

There's good news where gift tax is concerned, good news that provides you with a good opportunity to help your kids meet their financial goals. You can currently give up to $10,000 a year per individual in cash, securities, or other property without owing any gift tax or even filing a gift tax return. A couple can give $20,000 to an unlimited number of individuals, free of gift tax.

THE BOTTOM LINE ON FAMILY INVESTING

- *We are responsible for our children's financial education.*
- *As you develop your investing strategy, explain the issues and trade-offs to your family.*
- *If you invest the money intended for your children's future for long-term growth, it can match or outpace inflation.*

10

WHERE DO YOU GO FROM HERE?

So now what?

Hopefully you've decided to start or continue a regular investing program. But maybe you feel you need more help. If so, it's available in lots of places, but be careful where you look for it. What follows is information on two good sources: investment managers and investment clubs.

INVESTMENT MANAGERS

While it's my belief that managing your own investments isn't difficult or overly time consuming, there are times when you want professional help. Maybe you've recently taken control of a retirement distribution or received an inheritance. Or maybe you just feel that you don't have time to handle the day-to-day details of managing your money.

When should you consult an investment manager? There are several criteria, the first and most obvious having to do with the amount of money you want to invest. Because of the simple economics involved, it doesn't make sense to hire someone to manage your money unless you have a minimum of $100,000 to invest. If you're not in that category, you're better off doing the work yourself, plain and simple.

If you do have $100,000, you might consider an investment manager for several reasons. Lack of time is probably the most common. The need for expertise is another. If your financial situation is more complex than most, you may want professional help in mapping out a financial plan. Or maybe you just feel that there must be a better way to meet your financial goals, but you don't know what it is.

If professional money management looks like a good choice for you, the next step is to find the investment manager who suits your needs and fits your style. He or she will help you analyze your current needs, your long-term objectives, and your attitude toward risk, and determine the best investment plan to meet them. Then he or she will go into action and handle your day-to-day business for you: making investment decisions, monitoring your account, and keeping you updated. And you can feel confident that your finances are being managed by someone who understands your investment goals.

Most investment managers base their fees on a percentage of the assets they manage. (Typical annual fees range from 1% to 3% of the assets under their management.) This *fee-based management* is in your best interest, because your manager is paid based on the service he or she provides, rather than on the basis of trading commissions charged to your account. This means he or she is making recommendations and decisions with no conflict of interest. The investment decisions are guided by one primary goal—increasing your assets.

JOIN THE CLUB: THE INS AND OUTS OF INVESTMENT CLUBS

Investment clubs have become increasingly popular in recent years, thanks in large part to the success of the Beardstown Ladies

Investment Club. There's good reason for all the activity that clubs have sparked: They're a great way to invest. A lot of people find that they get better results when they invest as part of a club than they do individually. That makes sense. An investment club forces you to be more disciplined and more systematic than you might be on your own. The National Association of Investors Corporation (NAIC) states, "In any year, investment clubs beat the market about 60% of the time, whereas mutual funds beat it only 35% of the time."

Generally speaking, here's how an investment club works. Everyone agrees to invest the same amount of money at regular intervals, say, $35 a month. Clubs typically consist of 15 to 20 members who meet once a month to pick stocks and discuss the club's investments. Members vote on all investing decisions—what or when to buy and sell—and the majority vote wins. It's all pretty simple and straightforward, and it's often successful and fun to boot.

Investment clubs tend to invest in individual stocks; as one club member said, mutual funds are simply less fun to watch. Even though mutual funds are great investments, in a club environment they're less interesting. When it comes to picking individual stocks, clubs are usually pretty thorough. The research they do is key.

If you're interested in joining an investment club, the National Association of Investors Corporation is a good place to start. It's a good resource for both new and experienced investors, and a lot of people have found it helpful. NAIC has somewhere around 391,000 members—including about 64,000 individual members and about 25,000 member clubs—and it has been operating since 1941. It emphasizes much of what's been discussed in these pages—long-term, systematic investing, which it calls a "get-rich-slow program." Specifically, NAIC suggests that members invest a set amount regularly, reinvest dividends and capital gains, and invest in growth stocks of companies in different industries and of varying sizes.

NAIC members are very willing to share what they have learned about investing with others, through volunteers, seminars, and fairs, and their magazine, *Better Investing*. NAIC can also provide you with a list of regional contacts for existing clubs. (You can join as an individual or as part of a club.) If you want to start an investment club, NAIC can give you helpful information. It doesn't take a lot of money or experience to get started, and you can even think of it as giving something back, helping others get started on an investment program of their own. NAIC even offers investors' manuals, including a guide to starting a club, an accounting manual, and a guide to picking stocks. (You'll find contact information for NAIC in the Appendix.)

* * *

I'm a big supporter of investment clubs, but I confess that I don't have firsthand experience with one. Fortunately I know someone who does; my wife, Helen, has been in an investment club for ten years. What follows is her experience, in her own words.

▪ ▪ ▪ ▪ ▪ ▪ ▪ ▪ ▪ ▪ ▪ ▪ ▪ ▪ ▪ ▪ ▪ ▪ ▪ ▪

AN INVESTMENT CLUB FIRSTHAND: HELEN SCHWAB

People are usually surprised when they learn I'm in an investment club. "After all," they seem to be thinking, "you shouldn't have to worry about this stuff. You're married to someone who can handle it pretty well."

Well, yes, but that's missing the point, isn't it? It's true that I have someone at home who can handle it and is happy to do so, but that's really not the way I like to do things. Before I married Chuck, I was widowed at 25, and financial independence became very important to me. But the world of finance was a mystery, and *The Wall Street Journal* used a language I didn't know. Still, it all intrigued me. I found that investing was something I wanted to know more about and experience for myself.

So about ten years ago, when a close friend and I found ourselves talking about money and planning and finances, we realized that this was an area of our lives that was both interesting and important, and one that we didn't know nearly as well as we'd like to. The solution? We decided to start an investment club. If it sounds a little daunting—two women who were relatively inexperienced with investing just starting a club—well, it was at first.

We started by watching. The mother of a friend of ours belonged to an investment club in Hillsborough, California. The club was made up of women our mothers' ages, and it had been in existence for 15 years. We called one of the members and asked if we could attend a meeting just to observe. She agreed, and after we did, we were on our way, certain that this was what we wanted to do.

We had some ground rules to start, mostly from the Hillsborough group, suggestions that we followed and were glad we did. The list below gives some guidelines that have stood us well. Some of these things we were told, others we learned by doing.

Don't ask all (or only) your best friends to join. It turns the club into a social hour. A group of friends ignored this suggestion, and their club eventually disbanded because everybody just got together and talked and had a good time, and none of the business got done.

Ask members from different towns to join. In our case, this turned out to be three sections of the Bay Area: the Peninsula, Hillsborough, and San Francisco. Making sure that all the members aren't from the same town gives the club a little diversity and works against the club becoming too social. When we lose a member from one area, we choose a new member from the same area, so we stay geographically diverse.

Twenty members seems to be a good size. You need enough members to make a vote mean something, but more than twenty gets hard to handle. A smaller club places too much of the work on fewer shoulders.

While you don't want all the members to be in the same social circle, it's helpful if they share a certain commonality in experience and age. This was something we learned ourselves. Most of the women in that first club we watched were in their sixties; we formed our club when we were in our forties, and now we're in our fifties. And while the members obviously don't have to be lock-step in line with each other or exactly the same age, it does help to be at similar places in life. A lot of us, for example, have kids in college right now; and we're dealing with aging parents, or with the deaths of our parents. We're seeing the financial realities of our parents' lives, and sometimes we're even making life decisions for our parents. These are important life events, and they affect the way we think and feel and perceive the world.

The club agrees not to purchase stock in a company that employs any of the members or their spouses. This rule is in the interest of objectivity and fairness, and it seems to prevent a lot of potential difficulties. It's difficult to discuss selling a poor-performing stock if someone's husband works for the company.

The club functions well with three officers: a president, a vice-president, and a treasurer. Their terms are one year. Our president guides the group toward different industries, then we look at a number of good companies within those industries. The vice-president schedules periodic guest speakers and assigns stock reports to members. The job of treasurer is the most difficult because she takes care of all the trades, produces a monthly stock summary showing the price movement of each stock, and tracks our individual equity interest.

In 1986, armed with what we'd observed and whatever else we'd picked up from asking around, we formed our club, the Fortune Twenty, a group of women from the Bay Area. We found that other women were eager to join. A lot of them were like us, women who hadn't paid much attention to the financial part of their lives and wanted to be better informed. Some of us knew a little about investing, but many of us knew very little. One of our members had recently become a widow and had not even known which drawer to look in for the financial records after her husband's death.

At the start, we were all inexperienced at picking stocks. So we did what a lot of beginners do—we focused on just about every tip we got. Three things happened: We bought cheap, shot from the hip, and lost money like crazy. Finally, after about two years of frustration, we took a good look at our situation and said, "This is all wrong." We decided to try something else: *We decided to buy what we knew.*

We started to look around and talk about where we shopped, and what clothes our kids were wearing, and where we ate with them, and what we bought at the market. Names like Nordstrom and The Gap and McDonald's and Coca-Cola came up, and all of a sudden we saw that those weren't just names of stores or places or products. *They were names of companies,* corporations in which we could buy ownership, and a whole new world of investing began to emerge.

We were learning to sit up and take notice, to see the world through investors' eyes, and we took to it well. How to choose an industry? Once again, we simply paid attention. One member was using Retin-A to treat skin cancer and told us that it also worked on wrinkles; several of us knew something about hormone replacement therapy. Those things led to us looking at drug companies like Merck and Abbott Labs. We were concerned about the environment and conservation and the then-new rage for recycling, so we started talking about waste management. More companies—and more potential stocks.

But while we were learning how to notice the companies around us, we were also learning something even more valuable: the art of researching a stock. We didn't just pick these companies and buy according to our instincts. *Our interests were based on what we noticed, but our purchases were based on what we learned.*

We learned that the hard way. For a while we relied on word of mouth and did no research at all. We'd just ask someone who we thought knew something about the company or the market. But little by little we learned to do our homework—it's no fun to discover too late that you've purchased a stock near its all-time high. We eventually learned to examine the stock price of a company by using the *NAIC Stock Selection Guide.* We invited guest speakers to meetings, experts who knew about a specific industry or stock, and we'd hear that perspective. Then we became more independent: We learned to do the research ourselves. We had someone come and explain how to analyze a financial report, we learned about Value Line and *Daily Graphs,* and we were off and running.

Over the years, we've become more and more systematic. We meet once a month, except during July and August, on a Monday, at a member's home for lunch. A typical meeting lasts two hours. Once a year we discuss our goals. We have an agenda for each meeting. Guest speakers attend a few times a year—a stockbroker, or someone from a money management firm, or someone who can talk about a specific part of the process, like rebalancing your portfolio. In terms of buying stocks, five or six times a year we decide on an industry to focus on, then choose perhaps two of the leaders in that industry to research, and the members research those stocks thoroughly. This leaning toward industry leaders has given our portfolio a bit of a blue-chip bias, but that certainly doesn't seem like a negative. Our purchase decisions are made with great care; we're a long way from where we started. We have to vote on any trade, and that vote must pass with a quorum. At the start, we used a full-commission broker. Today the treasurer takes care of the trades herself, usually online or over the phone with our discount brokerage firm.

We very definitely follow a buy-and-hold strategy, and we sell only when it's warranted. Over the years two members have moved and we've had to sell something in order to buy them out, and a few times we've sold because we see evidence that a company is going downhill. And we sell when we see that a stock's really not performing well. But selling is the exception, and it is painful. These are, after all, good solid companies that we've chosen with great care. They're companies we've believed in, and it's difficult to walk away from something you've had confidence in. I am, very simply, just about always reluctant to sell.

And the rewards of all this? They are varied, but the financial ones are probably the most obvious. When we formed the Fortune Twenty in 1986, each member put in $500. Since then we've averaged $25 a month per member, pretty doable by most standards. And like many investors, we've seen that periodic regular investing smooths out the ups and downs of the market. The total amount I've invested is $3,075; today my shares are worth a total of $9,133, which means that I've tripled my money in eleven years. Not bad. In 1990 we owned stock in 9 companies. That number's now at 26.

There are other important rewards. The friendships that have developed are perhaps our biggest dividend, and we have the satisfaction of removing the mystery from this part of our lives. It feels good to pay attention to investing, but it's more important than just feeling good. Remember that woman who, when her husband died, didn't know which drawer held their financial records?

Today she reads *The Wall Street Journal* from cover to cover and is one of our most informed members. Another has written a book on getting your financial world in order. And virtually all of us now invest on our own as well as with the club.

Perhaps most important in all this is the reward of understanding the financial realities of our lives. What we have learned is this: *You have to be informed.* This is an area of your life where you cannot afford to be naive. You have to take charge.

■ ■ ■ ■ ■ ■ ■ ■ ■ ■ ■ ■ ■ ■ ■ ■ ■ ■ ■

THE BOTTOM LINE ON WHERE TO GO FROM HERE

- *It doesn't make sense to hire someone to manage your money unless you have a minimum of $100,000 to invest.*
- *Consider only fee-based investment managers, professionals who base their fees on a percentage of the assets they manage.*
- *To join or start an investment club, contact the National Association of Investors Corporation (NAIC).*

EPILOGUE

Dear Reader,

I cannot get these people out of my mind. You read about them in the newspaper more and more lately: people who have worked hard for most or all of their adult lives but have nothing to show for it in terms of retirement. It's a relatively new phenomenon, the result of diminishing Social Security and pension plans. Here they are in their sixties or seventies—or eighties—with financial pressures that they shouldn't have to shoulder. These elderly men and women are finding, at this late stage of their lives, that they have no financial safety net. They're truly on their own, in a very frightening way. And although I wouldn't know any of them if I passed them on the street, their stories have stayed with me—because what has happened to them, how they have ended up, is at the very heart of my passion about investing.

A recent national news story described a 73-year-old man who works stocking the shelves and delivering food for public schools. *Seventy-three years old*—and his retirement is not in sight. His wife's health is failing, and his job is hard on him physically, not to mention emotionally, and the more you learn of his story, the more wrenching it becomes.

He didn't set out to end up here. Thirty years ago he was a branch manager, with salary and commissions reaching to $500 a week, an income that was more than adequate. He and his wife and children lived in a home they'd built, and they even had some of the extras: a boat, a camper, a motor home, vacations. It was, in many ways, the good life.

But they had no pension, no savings, no retirement plan, and today, because of some harsh economic realities of our times, this man works at a job that pays six dollars an hour, a job younger men are turning down. Even with that, he doesn't have enough.

This is a not a man who was unemployed year after year, someone who just couldn't hold down a job. This is a man who had a good job but who has little to show for those years of hard work, and his story pulls at me. I even find it frightening, but fear isn't the reason I bring it up. What this story is about is *having enough,* and that gets at the heart of investing.

Investing isn't just about the stock market. It's not about asset allocation and pie charts and financial planning. *Investing is about your life* and being able to live the way you want to live. While this book and others on the shelf may seem like they're explaining a sequence of difficult tasks, what we're talking about are *tools* that open doors and give you choices. Investing is about money in the same way that school is about education. They both offer you choices.

The language of investing can disguise this. The word itself, *investing,* makes us think of stock certificates, financial reports, brokerage statements; it all seems so removed from the stuff of our daily lives—dinnertime, and the kids going to college, and retirement. But dinnertime and college for the kids and the rest of your life are *exactly* what investing is all about.

In these pages, you've seen how to begin or continue to invest for your future. *Start investing now,* you've read; *diversify; invest steadily; be patient; take the long view.* Discipline yourself to hold on to or add to your investments through down markets as well as up, and when you hit a down market, just make a cup of tea, or take a walk, or head to the driving range, whatever will settle your nerves and take your mind off the market. But don't panic—and don't sell. Cultivate patience, the art of hanging in there, but never confuse patience with complacency. Patience means not acting on emotion. Complacency means not acting at all.

Learn to keep a tight rein on your emotions. Whenever we get too excited about something, be it the tulip mania in Holland two hundred years ago or the more recent boom in computer stocks, we have to take a long step back and realize we're becoming dangerously emotional. And that's when we need to calm down. If you can achieve a detached, philosophical attitude in your approach to investing, you'll avoid a common pitfall: the crowd mentality, which causes people to jump in, no questions asked, then make ineffectual, fitful attempts at investing. What happens? They give up, and out of sheer frustration and failure, they sweep their investing concerns right under the rug and walk away.

Investing is a commitment. Sign it in stone, cross your heart, do whatever it takes to commit yourself to long-term investing. This is not about making money overnight, and you have to understand and accept that or you'll find yourself wanting to jump ship at the first sign of a down market. Instead, learn to close your eyes and resist the urge to sell; in other words, learn to ride through those down markets. Once you do, the next one won't be quite as bad, and the one after that will be a little better. But I have to be honest: It never gets easy. Every down market can rattle you, if you let it, whether you've been at this for five years or fifty. Those downward turns never quite lose their edge. The only antidote is a steeliness that, while it may not come naturally, will come if you're patient.

Most important, *this is not a game.* Investing isn't about chance or whims, and it's not about fooling around. It's about having enough for the rest of your life.

But don't be overwhelmed and feel as though you have to do everything in a day. You don't. We don't expect our children to mature overnight; we don't ask ourselves to become proficient at a new sport or skill in a day. Many of the important endeavors in life take time, and this one may take time as well. It's fine to let the investor side of you mature gradually.

Truth be told, we're all investors. Each day of our lives, we invest time and energy and intelligence in our children and our work. Investing for our future is just another aspect of it, but a crucial one.

So choose a starting place, and develop a plan to continue. You know how to get started. The only thing that remains is to begin. I wish you all the best as you set out.

Charles R Schwab

APPENDIX

WHERE TO LEARN MORE

Becoming a well-rounded investor simply means paying attention and gathering information. There are many resources for information. At a minimum, I'd suggest you use the Internet for timely information and become familiar with the financial pages of a daily newspaper and one or two investors' magazines. Beyond that, it's up to you.

ONLINE RESOURCES

Because of the very nature of the Internet, this list of suggested Web sites may be out of date after it appears. With that risk in mind, here are some general suggestions for places to start:

www.schwab.com
A personal favorite, and while I may be biased, I heartily recommend it. (Be sure to check out the index on Market Buzz.)

www.investorama.com
Short descriptions of thousands of links to investor sites.

www.investorguide.com
A massive site with a free e-mail newsletter.

investor.msn.com
Microsoft's investor site.

aaii.org/basics/invbasics.html
Investing basics from the American Association of Investors.

www.barrons.com
The site for *Barron's*, one of the nation's leading investment newspapers.

www.betterinvesting.org/clubs/thirteen.html
Everything you need to know about investment clubs.

www.bloomberg.com
Breaking financial news and up-to-date market information.

www.usatoday.com/news/comment/colwag.htm
Weekly column and Q&A with mutual fund guru John Waggoner.

www.vanguard.com
Vanguard's site, good for basic information.

www.sec.gov
The site for EDGAR, which stands for Electronic Data Gathering Analysis and Retrieval, a service of the Securities and Exchange Commission. Provides information about specific companies and financial reports that include net income, gross profit, debt, and acquisitions. Search for a company you like, then read its profile.

NEWSPAPERS

The Wall Street Journal	*The New York Times*
Investor's Business Daily	*The Los Angeles Times*
USA Today (financial section)	*The Chicago Tribune*

INVESTORS' MAGAZINES

Forbes	*Business Week*
Money	*Barron's*
Fortune	*Smart Money*

BOOKS

As anyone who's walked down the Personal Finance aisle of a bookstore or library knows, there are an astounding number of books available, and more every week. A lot of them are great, but some aren't much help. Herewith are my preferences:

The Basics

The best all-around, find-anything-you-need book that I've seen is *Making the Most of Your Money* by Jane Bryant Quinn. It's thorough and easy to read and understand, and it covers just about everything you can think of. It's a great reference book, a dictionary and encyclopedia of personal finance all in one. I highly recommend it.

Other good books covering the basics are Jeremy Siegel's *Stocks for the Long Run,* and just about anything by Peter Lynch, the former manager of the Fidelity Magellan Fund. *Personal Finance for Dummies* by Eric Tyson is easy to understand and won't overwhelm you. *Kids and Money* by Neale Godfrey is great for any parent concerned about his or her children's financial education. *The Whiz Kid of Wall Street's Investment Guide* by Matt Seto with Steven Levingston is advice from a kid. *The Neatest Little Guide to Mutual Fund Investing* by Jason Kelly is a thorough and accessible discussion of mutual funds. I have also enjoyed *The Intelligent Investor* by Benjamin Graham, *Investment Psychology Explained* by Martin Pring, and *Battle for Investment Survival* by Gerald Loeb.

There are plenty of books written about the abuses that customers have suffered at the hands of full-commission brokers. I found *Serpent on the Rock* by Kurt Eichenwald particularly interesting. *Walk Down Wall Street* by Michael Burton is also a good read.

You may find some of the classics interesting reading. A fairly unusual one, often available at libraries, is *Extraordinary Popular Delusions and the Madness of Crowds*, written in the 1850s, about the delusions of crowds through history. It analyzes the psychology of human movements, which of course is the basis of the psychology of the stock market. *Confessions of a Stock Market Operator,* written under a pen name by Jesse Livermore, the so-called boy wonder of the 1920s, is also interesting.

INFORMATION ON MUTUAL FUNDS

The best print source for complete fund information is *Morningstar Mutual Funds.* Published every two weeks, it itemizes each mutual fund's performance, risk, portfolio, operating history, and distribution information. It also offers interviews with fund managers and gives concrete advice on buying or avoiding particular funds. *Morningstar Mutual Funds* costs $425 per year. For more information, phone (800) 735-0700, write to Morningstar at 225 West Wacker Drive, Chicago, IL 60606, or contact them at www.morningstar.net.

There are hundreds of mutual fund newsletters and advisory services, and nearly all of them provide useful information for making purchase decisions. Many go a step further and aid you in switching among funds to capture trends. But be careful: Think of these services as guides, not oracles. Their publishers will deny that they offer advice, while telling you how well you'd have done if you'd followed it.

INFORMATION ON INDIVIDUAL COMPANIES

A wealth of information is available here too. Many magazines and newspapers publish analysts' reports on likely investments, economic trends, and developments in specific industries. Many quality investment reference books and newsletters provide information that is professional and free from conflict of interest. You don't have to rely on any single source. Several of them are free at your local library.

Value Line

The Value Line Investment Survey ranks high on my list of information. It's a comprehensive source of data about companies' finances. It also gives investment recommendations. In its major publication, a thick, black loose-leaf binder, Value Line rates stocks for safety and timeliness. *Safety* is Value Line's estimate of the likelihood that a stock's price will fall; *timeliness* is its counsel about buying a stock now. Value Line publishes outlooks for selected industries and updates its recommendations about particular companies.

For each stock, Value Line computes a "beta coefficient," a number that represents the movement of that stock's price in relation to the market. A beta coefficient of 1 indicates that the stock price parallels the general market. A beta greater than 1 indicates the stock is more volatile, up and down, than the market in general. A beta less than 1 indicates the stock is less volatile than the general market.

You can consult Value Line for information on companies within a desirable industry and compare their financial data and investment recommendations, paying attention to timeliness and safety. Value Line is on the expensive side, but low-cost introductory subscriptions are advertised. You can reach Value Line online at *www.value-line.com.* Their phone number is (800) 634-3583, and the address is 220 East 42nd Street, 6th floor, New York, NY 10017.

Standard & Poor's

Most libraries carry the extensive reference books of this financial publisher. They contain detailed descriptions of companies and industries, including financial histories, addresses, and so on. Experienced investors use *Standard & Poor's Stock Guide* for a quick review of a company's financial statistics. These reference tools don't provide recommendations themselves, but Standard & Poor's weekly 12-page publication called *The Outlook* covers major companies and ranks their appreciation potential and quality. It also discusses which industries are expected to outperform others and lists stocks that may be headed for superior performances. An annual subscription to *The Outlook* is $298. You can reach Standard & Poor by phone at (800) 221-5277, by mail at 65 Broadway, New York, NY 10006, and online at *www.stockinfo.standard&poor.com.*

Schwab's Company Profiles

For the investor who has found a potentially interesting company, Schwab will provide a four-page company profile. Using information compiled from independent sources, each profile gives a business description, charts of price history, and a summary of analysts' recommendations and earnings estimates. This is a handy resource if you look at specific stocks occasionally but don't need an expensive annual subscription. You can find profiles online at *www.schwab.com.*

Corporate Publications

Two corporate documents to consult when considering a stock are its yearly annual report and its Form 10-K. A well-done annual report summarizes data of the firm's past performance and contains a chairman's letter outlining the firm's business direction. The section titled "Management Discussion and Analysis" provides operating and financial information. Form 10-K is often a more direct document that specifies a firm's business and explains any material reasons why it might be troubled. EDGAR is a good online resource *(www.sec.gov);* you'll find information on this tool on page 214. Annual reports are also available by calling (800) 4-ANNUAL.

INFORMATION ON INVESTMENT CLUBS

The National Association of Investors Corporation (NAIC) is a good source of information on joining or starting an investment club. You can reach NAIC at 711 West Thirteen-Mile Road, Madison Heights, MI 48071, or by phone at (248) 583-6242.

FOR THE MORE SERIOUS INVESTOR

Daily Graphs

Daily Graphs contains a wealth of information about individual stocks. For each stock included, this publication charts its activity over the past year in two-week intervals. It provides quarterly sales and earnings with percentage changes and earnings estimates, and the latest news story on each stock. Stocks are classified according to industry with relative strength value to that group.

There are two editions of *Daily Graphs.* The NASDAQ/American Stock Exchange edition lists 680 NASDAQ leaders and 200 NASDAQ most-actives; it includes coverage on the leading American Exchange stocks. The New York Stock Exchange edition lists 1,600 common stocks. Write to P.O. Box 66919, Los Angeles, CA 90066-0919, or call (800) 472-7479.

The SRC Green Book of 5-Trend 35-Year Charts

This publication gives a very thorough look at a large number of companies, industry groups, and market averages over a long period of time through various economic conditions and historical events. The charts help you to follow a company's earnings, dividend, and price patterns, and you can quickly see where its stock stands today relative to points in its past. Write to Securities Research Company, Babson-United Building, 101 Prescott Street, Wellesley Hills, MA 02181-7528, or call (617) 235-0900.

GLOSSARY

THE LANGUAGE OF INVESTING

active management Management of a fund or investment that seeks to outperform one of the financial markets, using research and experience.

active market A market in which there is a great deal of trading activity. Because of the large number of transactions, active markets are characterized by liquidity. They tend to have narrower spreads between the bid and the ask price than do less active markets.

aggressive growth fund A mutual fund that seeks rapid capital growth, often from small or emerging growth companies.

American Stock Exchange (AMEX) A stock exchange whose companies are, in general, smaller than those traded on the New York Stock Exchange. The American Stock Exchange is located in downtown Manhattan.

annual report A financial statement issued each year by a corporation or mutual fund. It lists assets, liabilities, and earnings, as well as some historical information. Each of the company's shareholders receives a copy of the annual report. To request one, you can contact the company's shareholders' services department.

annuity A tax-deferred investment in which the policyholder makes lump-sum or installment payments to an insurance company, then receives income at retirement. Investments in annuities grow without income taxation until the earnings are withdrawn, allowing for greater accumulation over time. A fixed annuity pays a guaranteed rate set by the insurance company. A variable annuity allows the investor a wide selection of fund portfolios, with the opportunity to earn greater returns based on the performance of the underlying investments. In both types of annuity, the principal is guaranteed upon death; that is, regardless of the performance of the investment accounts you select, your beneficiaries are guaranteed to receive the account value of the annuity or the original deposit, whichever is greater. Certain costs are associated with annuities, which may include surrender charges and other expenses and fees, which can vary greatly from one company to another.

ask price The price at which you can buy shares in a security. This is also called a mutual fund's net asset value, or NAV per share. It includes front-end sales charges, if applicable; otherwise, for a no-load mutual fund, the ask price is the same as the NAV.

asked price The price at which a security is being offered for sale. If you are buying, you want to know the asked price. Also known as the "offer" or "ask."

asset A property that has monetary value, including personal assets, such as a house, a car, jewelry, and financial assets, such as savings and investments.

asset allocation The process of deciding how to divide your money among the three types of asset classes: stocks, bonds, and cash equivalents. How you make this decision is determined by your tolerance for risk and your time horizon.

asset allocation fund A mutual fund that features a mix of stocks, bonds, and cash equivalents to meet a specific growth objective.

The fund automatically and professionally reallocates an investor's money based on changing market conditions.

asset class One of the three major types of investments: stocks, bonds, and cash equivalents.

automatic investment plan (AIP) An agreement between you and a brokerage firm in which you authorize regular investments to be made through payroll deductions or automatic transfers from your checking account.

automatic reinvestment An agreement by which all dividends produced by your investments are reinvested—that is, they are used to buy more shares of the same or another investment.

back-end load A charge for redeeming your shares within the first few years. It is also called a contingent deferred sales charge because it's reduced with each passing year.

balanced fund A mutual fund that attempts to produce both income and growth (rather than one or the other) from a mix of stocks, bonds, and cash equivalents.

bear market A declining market, in which prices are falling because more people want to sell than to buy.

beta coefficient The ratio between the volatility of a stock or mutual fund's price and the volatility of the market in general. If the beta of a stock is greater than 1, that stock is expected to rise or fall more than the market. If the beta is below 1, the stock typically moves up and down less than the market as a whole. The S&P 500 Index has a beta of 1. Conservative investors typically consider investing in stocks that have a beta lower than 1.

bid and ask The buy and sell prices for securities, representing the spread in the market. You buy at the ask, and sell at the bid.

bid price The highest price anyone is willing to pay for the security at a given time. This is important to know when you are selling.

block An order or a transaction involving ten thousand or more shares, or shares in excess of $200,000 in value.

blue chip A common stock that is highly esteemed as an investment based on good earnings over a long period of time.

bond An IOU issued by the federal and/or a local government or a corporation, stating that you have loaned money to the borrower and that you will be paid back on a certain date and at a certain rate of interest. Most bonds pay interest semiannually. Others accrue interest and pay a lump sum at maturity. There are a number of different types of bonds to choose from, with varying degrees of risk: corporate bonds, municipal bonds, government bonds, and unit investment trusts. Bond mutual funds are also available.

corporate bond A bond issued by a corporation as an alternative financing approach to issuing stock. Interest is usually paid semiannually, and the full principal is usually returned at maturity, which ranges from 1 to 30 years. A lot of people view corporate bonds as a more dependable investment than stock in the same company because companies pay interest and principal to bondholders before they pay dividends to stockholders; as such, these bonds seem like more of a sure thing. *Junk bonds* offer higher interest but carry a higher risk of default as well. *Investment grade bonds* offer lower interest than junk bonds but with presumably less risk. (The specifics of bonds vary, depending on the terms and conditions specified for a particular bond.)

municipal bond A bond issued by a state or local government or agency. Sometimes called "munis," they usually pay interest at a fixed rate semiannually and promise to return your entire principal at maturity.

The attraction of municipal bonds is that they offer tax-free income: The interest is free from federal taxation. If the municipal bond is issued from your own state of residence, the interest may be exempt from state and local taxes as well. As a result, munis are popular with investors in high tax brackets, because they can provide better after-tax yields than other fixed-income investments. But you have to be in the highest income tax brackets to really derive an advantage from the tax exemptions of municipal bonds. There are other drawbacks as well: if you need to sell, there may be a liquidity problem. And if you hope to get the best buys, you have to compete against the professionals.

government bond A bond issued by the U.S. Treasury or other agency. Everyone views U.S. government securities as the safest investments. An investment in a Treasury bill, note, or bond is backed by the full faith and credit of the U.S. government, so if you hold the investment until maturity, the possibility of losing the face value of the money you invest is zero. But a Treasury investment can be risky because market rates may rise above the fixed rate on your investment. Government bonds are exempt from state and local taxes.

There are several kinds of government investments. Treasury notes and bonds are intermediate and long-term investments that pay a fixed rate of interest semiannually and return their face value at maturity. The minimum investment is $5,000 for short-term notes and $1,000 for longer-term notes and bonds. The Treasury Department offers new bills, notes, and bonds at regularly scheduled auctions throughout the year. The price is set by auction bidding; you find out the price and interest rate you receive after you place your order. You can also place orders for new Treasuries through brokerage firms, government securities dealers, and some banks. It's also possible to place them directly with the Federal Reserve, though I don't recommend it because you may have to pay an account fee. Also, you'll be locked in—a Treasury held at the Federal Reserve can't be sold in the secondary market, so you have to hold it until maturity. It's better to use your brokerage firm or bank.

There is a secondary market for Treasury notes and bonds

as well. You can buy previously issued Treasury notes and bonds through brokerage firms and some banks. Secondary market availabilities are published daily in the financial press, which lists notes and bonds by maturity date and gives price and yield information. The advantages of buying them this way are that you have a wide choice of maturities and interest rates, and you can buy at any time, instead of exclusively at scheduled auctions.

Zero-coupon Treasuries (STRIPS) are issued by the U.S. Treasury at a deep discount from face value, with interest paid as a lump sum at maturity. They are pretty good time-specific investments because of their predictability and their high quality. If you need highly precise and punctual accumulations, you may want to consider zero-coupon bonds. Unlike conventional bonds, which pay interest in twice-yearly checks, zeros are sold at a deep discount from their face value, and they pay interest as the difference between purchase price and par (the face value). For example, you might pay $300 for a zero maturing in 12 years. At the end of 12 years, you receive $1,000, of which $700 is "accreted interest." During the intervening years, you receive nothing.

A disadvantage of zeros is the phenomenon called "phantom interest." Even though you don't receive interest until your zeros mature, the IRS demands that you declare interest yearly. You can overcome this problem by holding Treasury and corporate zeros in tax-deferred IRAs and Keoghs (but don't buy municipal zeros for this purpose, since they are not federally taxed anyway). Also, the market price of zeros can swing sharply when economywide interest rates change. Such sweeping price changes can be unsettling, but they shouldn't bother buy-and-hold investors who seek accumulations at maturity from quality zeros. A more worrisome issue with zeros is your greater exposure to price risk and inflation risk. As with all bonds, inflation erodes zeros' purchasing power at maturity. But inflation also generates higher interest rates, which drives the prices of zeros down.

bond fund A mutual fund that includes only bonds—typically corporate, municipal, or U.S. government bonds.

bond maturity The lifetime of a bond, concluding when the final payment of that obligation is due.

broker dealer A securities firm that sells mutual funds or other securities.

brokerage account An account with a brokerage firm that allows you to buy and sell securities.

bull market A rising market, in which prices are going up because more people want to buy than sell. A bullish investor believes that prices are going up and buys aggressively in anticipation of a market advance.

buy-and-hold An investing strategy that encourages investing for the long term by buying and then "holding," rather than selling based on the market's day-to-day ups and downs. Buying and then trying to sell based on the movement of the market is the opposite investment strategy and is called "market timing."

capital appreciation The growth of the principal of your investments.

capital gain The profit you receive when you sell an investment for more than you paid for it. Capital gains are taxable income and must be reported to the IRS on your tax return.

capital gains distribution A payment you receive when your mutual fund makes a profit by selling some of the securities in its portfolio. Capital gains distributions are usually made annually, often at the end of the calendar year.

capital growth An increase in the market value of a security, as reflected by the appreciation of the security's net asset value per share. Capital growth and income are the two major long-term goals of mutual funds.

capital loss The amount of money you lose when you sell an investment for less than you paid. Capital losses may be deducted from your annual income and must be reported on your tax return.

capital return The capital gain or loss realized from the market appreciation or depreciation of your investment. For example, if you purchased stock for $1,000 and sold it for $1,500, your capital gain would be $500.

capitalization For a specific company, the total stock market value of all shares of that company's stock.

cash account A brokerage account in which transactions are settled on a cash basis.

certificate of deposit (CD) A type of investment made with a financial institution, such as a bank or savings and loan. You deposit a specified amount for a specified period of time, at a preset, fixed interest rate. CDs are FDIC-insured.

closed-end mutual fund A mutual fund that distributes a fixed number of shares that trade much like stocks. They are usually listed on a major exchange, and they may trade in the market at a premium or discount to net asset value (NAV).

commission The fee paid to a brokerage firm for executing a trade.

commodities Goods such as agricultural products, like wheat or pork bellies, or metals, or financial instruments, traded on a separate commodities exchange. Commodity contracts state a future date of delivery or receipt of a certain amount of the product. Speculators generally invest in these contracts at a price that they hope they can turn into a profit when the actual commodities are delivered.

common stock Securities that represent an ownership interest in a corporation. The difference between common and preferred stock is that holders of preferred stock usually receive preferential treatment. For example, dividends must be paid on preferred stock, while dividend payment on common stock is optional. But preferred stocks pay a fixed dividend and may not change in value at the same rate as common stock.

compounding Generally speaking, the growth that results from investment income being reinvested. Compound growth has a snowball effect because both the original investment *and the income from that investment* are reinvested.

cost basis An investment's original cost. This number, which is used for tax purposes, includes any dividends that have been reinvested, and any capital gains distributions. To determine the capital gain or loss from the sale of an investment, subtract the cost basis from the sales price. (Sales price minus cost basis equals capital gain or loss.)

country risk The potential for fluctuation in the price of a stock sold in a foreign country. Fluctuations may have a variety of causes, such as political or financial events.

credit risk The possibility that the issuer of a bond—the borrower—will fail to repay the principal or interest owed on a bond, either at the agreed-upon time or at all—in other words, default. Also called "default risk."

currency risk The possibility that the price in dollars of an international stock may fluctuate as a result of changing currency exchange rates.

current yield The amount of annual interest on a bond divided by the amount paid for it, expressed as a percentage. For example, if you receive $80 a year from a bond that has a current price of $900, the current yield is 8.9% ($80 divided by $900).

custodial account An account set up and managed by an adult for the benefit of a minor. It is set up in the name of a child, with a parent or trustee as custodian. Assets placed in the account are considered an irrevocable gift and belong solely to the child. The custodian is entrusted with control of the account assets and is responsible for investing prudently on the child's behalf. The custodian manages the assets until the child reaches the age of majority, usually 18 or 21 (depending on the state law governing the custodial account). Once the child reaches this age of majority, he or she will take full control of the assets in the account. If you are opening a custodial account in a state governed by the Uniform Transfers to Minors Act, it's important to specify the age at which you wish the child to take possession of the account assets. Otherwise the assets will automatically transfer to the child when he or she turns 18 or 21, depending on his or her state of residence, or the state where the account was established, or both. On reaching the age of majority—often just when the need for college tuition is greatest—the child will receive all the assets in the account. Nearly every bank and brokerage firm offers custodial accounts.

day order An order to buy or sell a security that remains valid until executed or canceled by the customer. At the day's market close, if the order has not been executed or canceled by the customer, it is canceled automatically.

defined benefit plan A company retirement plan in which the employee, after retirement, receives a fixed amount of money on a regular basis from the employer—that is, a pension. The employer is responsible for investing. If you have a defined benefit pension plan, when you retire you will receive a fixed amount of money on a regular basis from your former employer. To learn how much the monthly benefit will be, ask your employer's plan manager, or review the plan summary, which you are entitled to receive by law. You'll need the information for planning your own retirement investment program.

defined contribution plan A company retirement plan in which an individual's retirement benefit is based on the amount contributed to the employee's account (plus earnings) by both the employee and the employer. Defined contribution plans include 401(k) or 403(b) plans, in which the employee elects to defer salary into the plan and directs the investments of the deferral. The company matches a part or all of the employee's contribution.

discount broker A brokerage firm that executes orders to buy and sell at commission rates that are lower than those of a full-commission brokerage firm.

diversification The allocation of investment money among multiple investments to spread risk, so that you own a mixture of different securities. Diversification is important to help cushion you against an unexpected price decline of any one or a few of your investments.

dividend The part of the income earned by a company issuing stock that is distributed to shareholders.

dividend reinvestment program (DRP) The automatic reinvestment of your dividends from a stock in more shares of that stock.

dollar cost averaging Investing the same dollar amount in securities at scheduled intervals over the long term.

Dow Jones Industrial Average One of the most commonly used measurements of the U.S. stock market. The Dow Jones Industrial Average was created by two reporters, Charles Dow and Eddie Jones, who started publishing *The Wall Street Journal* in 1889. From the start, their newspaper reported financial news, gave compilations of the stock prices of the larger important companies, and created indexes to track the performance of the stock market as a whole. Today's Dow Jones Industrial Average follows 30 large companies headquartered in the United States. They are not necessarily the best or largest companies in the country; they are, according to *The Wall Street Journal*, representative of the U.S. stock market. The list can change over time, as a result of mergers and changes in the performance of those companies.

earnings A company's revenue, after related costs and expenses have been deducted.

earnings per share (EPS) A company's net income, minus preferred dividends, divided by its number of common shares outstanding.

EDGAR An acronym for Electronic Data Gathering Analysis and Retrieval, an online service of the Securities and Exchange Commission (*www.sec.gov*). It offers information about specific companies, including financial sheets that show net income, gross profit, debt, and acquisitions.

emerging markets fund A mutual fund that invests chiefly in developing economies. These funds are often volatile, and their values can fluctuate substantially.

employee stock ownership plan (ESOP) A company retirement plan that invests in and pays benefits in the form of company stock instead of cash contributions.

equity Another name for stock. Also, the money value of a property or of an interest in a property in excess of all claims or liens against it.

equity income fund A mutual fund that pursues current income by investing at least 65% of its assets in dividend-paying equity securities.

ex-dividend For stocks, the period between the announcement of a dividend and payment of that dividend. When a stock is trading ex-dividend, new buyers do not receive the dividend. An "x" in newspaper listings denotes a stock that is ex-dividend.

expense ratio For mutual funds, the percentage of a fund's average net assets that are used to pay fund expenses. This percentage accounts for management fees, administrative fees, and any 12b-1 fees.

face value The value appearing on the face of a bond, indicating the principal amount that the issuer will pay when the bond matures and the amount on which interest is calculated. Face value is not an indication of market value.

FDIC An acronym for the Federal Deposit Insurance Corporation, a U.S. government agency that insures cash deposits, including certificates of deposit, that have been placed in member institutions, for up to $100,000 for each institution.

financial aid Assistance in paying for college costs. Grantors of financial aid typically require that a larger percentage of the assets held in the child's name be contributed toward college than the parents' assets. As a unique payment option, many colleges offer prepaid tuition plans. Basically, you pay years in advance for your youngster's later education. The state or the college invests the money and guarantees college costs for the child. The tax consequences and refund policies vary by institution and state.

fixed-income investment An investment that produces a constant rate of interest income, even if the market value of the principal amount changes. Most fixed-income securities produce a steady stream of semiannual interest payments. But some pay interest monthly, and a few pay no interest at all until the issue matures. As the term *fixed income* implies, the interest rate on most of these investments is fixed at the time the security is issued and remains constant throughout the life of the loan. The most common fixed-income investments are bonds. (See "bond" for more information.)

As with all investments, the after-tax returns on fixed-income securities are what count, so your income tax bracket will influence the kinds of investments you choose. Interest is taxed as ordinary income, so if you're in a high tax bracket, investments with tax advantages may be more attractive to you than fully taxable ones.

The chart shows the tax status of various types of fixed-income investments:

TAX STATUS OF FIXED-INCOME INVESTMENT TYPES

INVESTMENTS THAT OFFER INCOME THAT IS EXEMPT FROM FEDERAL AND/OR STATE TAXES:	INVESTMENTS THAT OFFER TAXABLE INCOME:
Municipal bonds	U.S. government securities
Municipal bond funds	Treasury bills, notes, and bonds
Municipal preferreds	Zero-coupon Treasuries (STRIPS)
Unit investment trusts (UITs)	U.S. government agency securities
Tax-exempt money funds	Certificates of deposit (CDs)
	Commercial paper
	Corporate bonds
	Investment-grade bonds
	High-yield bonds
	Mortgage-backed securities
	Ginnie Maes, Fannie Maes, Freddie Macs
	Money market funds
	Bond mutual funds
	Unit investment trusts (UITs)

401(k) plan A type of salary deferral plan that permits employees to make pretax contributions, reducing their taxable income. Employers can match some or all employee contributions.

403(b) plan A qualified retirement plan designed for nonprofit organizations. Employers can match some or all employee contributions.

front-end load A sales commission, or load, that you pay when you purchase shares of some mutual funds. It can be as high as 8.5% of the purchase amount ($85 on a $1,000 buy-in) but is more typically 4% to 6%.

fund family A group of mutual funds from the same organization. Investing in funds from the same fund family usually gives you exchange privileges between the funds, and you receive one statement for all of the funds in the family.

global fund A mutual fund that invests in both U.S. and non-U.S. companies. Typically 20% to 50% of the money is in U.S. equities. By contrast, an *international fund* invests only in foreign companies.

good-till-canceled (GTC) A limit order that a customer places with a brokerage firm to buy or sell stock; it remains valid until executed or canceled by the customer. At Schwab, all GTC orders that are not executed or canceled by the customer will automatically expire 60 days after the date the order is taken. Unlike a day order, a GTC order can be executed over several days.

growth and income fund A mutual fund that seeks both capital appreciation (growth) and current income. Stocks are selected based on both their appreciation potential and their ability to pay dividends.

growth fund A mutual fund that pursues capital appreciation by investing in equity securities. Current income is a secondary concern, if a concern at all.

growth stock The stock of a company that has previously seen rapid growth in revenue or earnings and is expected to see similar growth beyond the short term. Generally speaking, growth stocks pay relatively low dividends and sell at a relatively high price, considering their earnings and book value.

income fund A mutual fund that seeks current income over capital growth, often by investing in bonds and high-yielding stocks.

index A group of securities considered yardsticks of market behavior. Well-known market indexes include the Standard & Poor's 500 Index, the Dow Jones Industrial Average, and the Schwab 1000.

index mutual fund A mutual fund that seeks to replicate the performance of an established index. Investing in an index fund gives you a way to participate in an overall market while diversifying your portfolio.

inflation risk The possibility that increased inflation—an increase in the cost of living—will reduce or eliminate a specific investment's returns.

interest Payments made to compensate an investment at a fixed percentage rate during each year the investment is owned. For bonds, payments are usually made semiannually.

interest rate return The percentage of a bond's value that will be paid to the bondholder periodically until it matures. For example, a $1,000 bond with an interest rate of 7% would pay you $70 a year (7% × $1,000). Often referred to as "coupon rate."

interest rate risk The possibility that the value of an investment will decrease as a result of changes in market interest rates.

international fund A mutual fund that invests only in foreign companies and holds no stock in U.S. companies (as opposed to a global fund, which invests in both U.S. and non-U.S. companies, with typically 20% to 50% of the money in U.S. equities). International funds generally concentrate on stocks in Europe, emerging markets, or the Pacific Rim. They can also specialize by investing exclusively in companies from a specific region (like Europe, the Pacific Rim, or Latin America) or a specific country (like Japan), hoping to capitalize on those areas that will see the most growth. Other international funds invest in the securities of emerging markets, or developing foreign countries. Their investment objective is usually long-term growth.

investment club A group of people who agree to pool their money and invest as a club. Each person invests the same amount of money at regular intervals, say, $35 a month; the amount varies, as does the interval. Clubs typically comprise 15 to 20 members, and they usually meet once a month to pick stocks and discuss the club's investments. Members vote on all investing decisions— what to buy, and what or when to sell—and majority vote wins.

IPO (initial public offering) A private company whose shares are being offered to the public for the first time. Also called a "new issue."

IRA (individual retirement account) A retirement account that provides tax benefits. The money you invest in an IRA is *tax-deferred*, meaning that you don't pay taxes on it until you withdraw it during your retirement. Free of the yearly tax setback, the investment you make in an IRA may grow bigger and faster. Every year you can invest up to $2,000 of the money you earn from wages or salary in an IRA—$4,000 if you're married and your spouse is not a wage earner, $4,000 if you and your spouse are each earning at least $2,000. You may also get a current-year tax deduction for your IRA contributions, depending on your income level and your participation in other pension plans.

Because capital gains and income taxes are deferred until a distribution is taken, an IRA can shelter investments that potentially will produce high growth and high earnings.

IRA rollover A tax-free transfer of assets from one qualified plan to another. Also called a "conduit IRA."

If you change jobs, retire, or get a divorce settlement that includes a distribution from a company retirement plan, you can "roll it over" into an IRA to preserve your capital and keep it growing free of current-year taxes. Your distribution will be subject to an automatic 20% withholding for income tax unless your old employer rolls it over directly from your current plan into the new plan. To roll your distribution over directly, your check or electronic transfer must be made payable to the sponsor of your IRA (or the trustee of your new employer's retirement plan for your benefit).

If your old employer made your distribution directly to you, you must deposit the funds into a rollover IRA (or your new employer's retirement plan) within 60 days from the date of the distribution to avoid current-tax liabilities. If your assets are not transferred within the 60-day limit, they become current income for tax purposes and in most cases carry a 10% additional penalty if you are under $59^1/_2$ years old. Your employer will be required to withhold 20% of your payout, so you will only get 80%. In order to avoid paying taxes on the 20%, you will need to make it up out of other funds and roll over all the rest of your distribution into an IRA. You can then request a refund of the withheld taxes, but this is an undesirable approach.

irrevocable living trust A legal agreement to transfer funds from a donor to a beneficiary through a trust that generally offers tax advantages. An irrevocable living trust may offer more flexibility than a direct gift because you can specify a purpose for which the funds may be used and the date when your child will receive the assets. This type of plan, set up with an attorney, allows you to specify how much of the account assets will be distributed to your child and at what specific period(s). Irrevocable trusts are beneficial in limited situations and can have complex tax ramifications. It's important to consult an attorney when considering this option.

issuer The corporation, municipality, or government agency that issues a bond or security.

junk bond A high-yield security that can involve a substantial risk. Such bonds are not considered investment grade and are rated below BB. A *junk bond fund* invests in these bonds.

Keogh plan An employer-sponsored retirement plan for a partnership (or for a sole proprietorship for self-employed people). It requires significantly more paperwork than an IRA, and it's more complex to understand and manage. You may want to meet with a financial adviser to discuss Keogh plans in detail.

Although it works like an IRA, a Keogh plan can permit self-employed individuals to make higher tax-deductible contributions. Keogh plans must be adopted before the end of the business tax year—usually December 31. Contributions can be made up to the time for filing the employer's federal income tax return, including extensions. If you have eligible employees, you must make contributions for them at the same rate that you use for your own contributions.

large capitalization stock The stock of a company with a market value of over $10 billion. Large cap companies are well-established, with solid track records of steady growth and dividend payments.

life insurance An integral part of a financial plan. Life insurance guarantees cash when it's needed most, so that the policyholder's survivors can replace income, pay off a home, fund children's education, or cover an unexpected financial obligation. Life insurance can also help you preserve your estate and allow it to pass to your heirs intact, protecting it from estate taxes. This is especially important if your estate consists of illiquid assets such as real estate or a family business.

Choosing a good insurance company is crucial—and often difficult. Key factors are a company's superior financial strength, stability, and top ratings within the industry. You can check the ratings in several areas—like financial strength, operating performance, ability to meet policyholder obligations, and claims-paying ability—with rating services such as A. M. Best Company, Standard & Poor's, Duff & Phelps, and Moody's Investor Service.

Once you've chosen a company, you need to choose the type of policy you want. Each type of insurance offers different features and benefits. *Permanent* or *whole life insurance* stays in effect until the death of the policyholder and should be avoided. *Term insurance* stays in effect for only a specified time period, or until the policyholder reaches a certain age. Then the policyholder can renew it, at a higher premium. Unlike permanent life insurance, term insurance policies have no interest-bearing account or cash value. Term insurance offers the maximum amount of coverage for the lowest premium. Key features to look for are premium guarantees, convertibility, renewability, and reentry. *Universal life insurance* is designed to provide permanent protection, flexible premiums, and cash values. These policy cash values can accumulate, tax-deferred, to offset premiums, or they can be drawn against to provide tax-favored income. The premiums are generally higher than for term insurance, but they can remain level for life. *Survivorship universal life insurance* is similar but covers two lives and is payable after the death of the second insured person. It is most often used to cover estate taxes. Key features to look for when evaluating universal life and survivorship universal are sales loads, surrender charges, and cash values.

When choosing your policy, ask for *guaranteed annual renewable* term insurance. Such a policy will let you remain insured indefinitely, regardless of changes in your medical condition. These kinds of policies are inexpensive, and the more insurance you buy, the lower the rate.

Determining the amount of life insurance you need isn't easy. Everyone's situation is unique and depends on factors such as age, number of dependents, and financial profile. If you're single and have no one dependent on you, all you need is burial insurance and enough to pay off your debts. If you're married or divorced and supporting children, you can use any of several methods to come up with an amount. In general, people base the amount of coverage they need on one of the following:

1. A multiple of their income. This is the simplest—and probably the least accurate—way to arrive at a figure. It is a general rule of thumb that says your life insurance coverage should be 8 to 12 times your annual income. If your annual income is $50,000 and you have one child, you may want to buy $400,000 to $600,000 of coverage, taking into account any special needs and existing coverage.

2. Income replacement and investment return. This method figures you need enough coverage so that the death benefit,

invested at a high yield, will replace your income. For example, if you need to replace a $76,000 income, and you feel that 8% is a realistic return on investments, then you would purchase $950,000 of coverage ($950,000 × 8% = $76,000). This amount would allow you to retain the principal intact. If you believe you will receive a higher investment return, you can reduce the amount of insurance; if you believe you will receive a lower return, increase the amount.

3. Goals and current assets. This method weighs your specific needs and goals against your assets and liabilities to arrive at a more customized figure. Estimate your survivors' immediate cash needs at your death (for example, administration expenses, debts, and loans) and their future cash needs (including family income, education fund, and spousal retirement fund); then subtract the value of your total assets (cash, savings, employee benefits) from that amount. That total is the coverage you would need.

For a more extensive discussion of insurance, see Jane Bryant Quinn's *Making the Most of Your Money.*

limit order An order to buy or sell a security at a specified price or better. A limit order to buy sets a maximum purchase price. A limit order to sell sets a minimum sale price.

liquid investment An investment that can be easily converted to cash.

liquidity How quickly you can convert an investment into cash.

load A onetime sales commission that is assessed by some mutual funds to compensate the broker or financial planner who sells them. The most common types of loads are front-end (assessed when you purchase the fund) and back-end (assessed when you sell the fund). Loads typically range from 3% to 8.5%.

load fund A mutual fund that assesses a sales charge or commission.

long-term capital gain A profit you make after selling a stock or mutual fund that you have owned for more than one year.

management fee The amount a mutual fund pays its investment adviser to manage the fund.

margin account A type of brokerage account that allows certain securities to be used as collateral for a loan. You will be able to use margin after signing a margin agreement and meeting regulatory requirements. All trades using borrowed money will be conducted through the margin account.

marginal tax rate The tax rate you pay on your last dollar of income, or the amount of tax imposed on an additional dollar of income.

market capitalization The total value of a company's stock, calculated by multiplying the number of shares outstanding by the current market price per share.

market order An order to buy or sell a security at the best price available at the time the order is received. During market hours, only limit, stop, and stop-limit orders can be changed, because market orders are usually executed too quickly.

market value For a stock, the total number of shares outstanding multiplied by the price per share.

maturity date The date when the principal amount of a fixed-income investment is payable by the issuer.

money market fund A mutual fund that invests solely in short-term (less than one year) securities with high liquidity—that is, securities that are easily turned into cash. Examples of short-term securities include Treasury bills, certificates of deposit (CDs), and short-term loans.

mortgage-backed bond A bond that represents an interest in and pays interest from a pool of mortgages.

municipal bond An obligation of a state, city, town, school district, or public authority. In general, interest paid on municipal bonds is exempt from federal taxes.

mutual fund An investment company that pools the money of many investors and buys various securities (such as shares of stock in many companies or various bonds). Investors who own shares of the mutual fund automatically achieve the safety of a diversified portfolio without having to buy the individual investments themselves. What this means is that through one investment, you can own stock in hundreds of companies, giving you diversification. (See also "prospectus.")

NASDAQ An acronym for National Association of Securities Dealers Automated Quotations. A computerized system for reporting current price quotations on active over-the-counter securities. The system provides price quotations and permits execution of small customer orders. Large orders are executed by separate negotiations.

National Association of Investors Corporation (NAIC) An organization that provides information and support for both new and experienced investors. It has somewhere around 391,000 members and has been operating since 1941. The organization advances what it calls a "get-rich-slow program of long-term investing." It suggests that members invest a set amount regularly, reinvest dividends and capital gains, and invest in growth stocks of companies in different industries and of varying sizes. You can reach NAIC at 711 West Thirteen-Mile Road, Madison Heights, MI 48071, or by phone at (248) 583-6242.

net asset value (NAV) The market value of a single share of a mutual fund. It is calculated at the end of each business day by adding up the value of all the securities in the fund's portfolio, subtracting expenses, and dividing the sum by the number of shares outstanding.

net profit The remaining profit on an investment, once you've deducted all expenses.

net worth The total value of all of the assets you own, once you've deducted any outstanding debts.

New York Stock Exchange (NYSE) The oldest and largest stock exchange in the United States. Founded in 1792, the NYSE is located at 11 Wall Street in New York City. It is governed by a 20-member board of directors (approximately half of whom represent the public and half of whom represent the exchange membership) with a full-time, paid chairman.

no-load mutual fund A mutual fund that charges no dealer or underwriting fee or commission, either at the time of purchase or at the time of sale. Its shares are sold at the fund's net asset value.

odd lot A trade involving less than 100 shares.

offering price the purchase price per share of a mutual fund. This is determined by adding any sales charges that apply to the fund's net asset value per share. Also called *ask price.*

open-end mutual fund A mutual fund that continuously sells its shares to the general public without the need for fixed capitalization. An open-end fund issues additional shares as new investors ask to buy them. The number of shares outstanding therefore changes daily as investors buy new shares or redeem old shares. The market price of a share in an open-end fund can't fall below NAV because funds redeem their shares at NAV. The offering price will exceed NAV, however, when there is a load or sales charge. Shares of a no-load fund are bought directly from the fund and carry no sales charge, or through a brokerage firm that may charge a transaction processing fee.

open order A buy or sell order that has not yet been executed or canceled.

operating expense ratio (OER) A mutual fund's annual expenses (operating expenses, management fees, and 12b-1 fees, if any) expressed as a percentage of the fund's average net assets. These expenses are deducted before calculating the fund's NAV.

option An option is a contract that allows an investor to control 100 shares of stock for a pre-agreed period of time. Many brokerages offer index and listed stock options on all of the major exchanges. But options aren't suitable for all investors, and because they carry a relatively high level of risk, you usually have to be approved by your brokerage firm to trade them. If you are approved to trade options, you'll need to do the following (in addition to giving your account number) with your broker when you trade: Specify puts or calls; opening or closing a position; number of contracts; underlying stock or index; and expiration month(s) and strike price(s).

over the counter (OTC) A market of securities that are not listed on an exchange but trade only in the over-the-counter network (via telephone or a computer network, instead of an exchange floor).

par For common stocks, the dollar value assigned to the stock when the stock is issued. Par value is used chiefly for bookkeeping, rather than for figuring the stock's market value. For preferred stocks, par is the amount used to calculate the investor's dividend. For a bond, the par value is the face amount—the amount the issuer has agreed to pay at maturity.

penny stock A low-priced stock, generally selling below one dollar per share. The SEC has defined penny stocks as those with a value of less than five dollars and that do not meet certain asset or other requirements. Penny stocks do not include listed securities, National Market System securities, or mutual fund securities, even where they are priced under five dollars. The term is something of a misnomer.

point A one-dollar change in a stock's market price. If a stock is up 10 points, its price has increased by $10.

portfolio The securities held by an investor; that is, the investments (stocks, bonds, and cash equivalents) that you own. Also, the securities that a mutual fund holds.

portfolio manager The person in charge of managing a mutual fund's holdings.

preferred stock A class of stock that has a claim on the company's earnings before payment is made on the common stock if the company declares a dividend. (See also "common stock.")

price/earnings ratio (P/E) A stock's current price divided by its earnings of the past year. A stock's P/E is an indicator of the market's expectations about that stock. A higher P/E means higher expectations for the company's growth in earnings.

prime rate The interest rate charged by banks for the customers they deem most creditworthy, or prime.

principal The amount of money that is financed, borrowed, or invested. For a bond, the face value, payable at maturity.

prospectus A legal statement that describes the objectives of a specific investment. Every mutual fund is required to publish a prospectus and to give investors a copy, free of charge. To get one, just call the fund itself. You should look for the following in a prospectus:

The fund's investment objectives. Make sure at the start that the fund's investment goals are in keeping with your own investment goals and with your tolerance for risk. With mutual funds as with other investments, the higher the risk, the greater the potential reward. You can learn about a mutual fund's investment strategy through its prospectus, which outlines the fund's objectives.

The kind of securities the fund holds. The portfolio may include money market securities, bonds, stocks, precious metals, options, warrants, and hedge transactions. You may already know this before you read the prospectus, but it's wise to double-check and make sure the fund is investing in what you think it is.

Investment minimums. A stock fund usually requires an initial investment of $1,000 to $5,000. Subsequent purchases have lower minimums, often $50 to $500.

Sales charges and fees. Make sure the fund is no-load. A true no-load fund (which is what you want) imposes no front- or back-end sales charges. (See "front-end load" and "back-end load.")

Every mutual fund, whether load or no-load, charges an annual fee to pay its portfolio manager and cover other fund expenditures. This fee is quoted as a percentage of the fund's average annual assets and is often called the fund's operating expense ratio. In addition, some funds take an extra bit to cover the fund's advertising and promotion expenses. Called a 12b-1 fee after the regulation authorizing it, this fee has no regulatory cap; some funds charge 1 percent or more. These fees are not paid directly by the shareholder but are taken out of the fund's current income before distribution to the shareholder. So the lower the fund's fees, the more the shareholder benefits.

How often earnings are distributed. Funds distribute dividends and realized capital gains either monthly, quarterly, semiannually, or yearly. It may not be a good idea to invest in a stock fund late in the year, since you could receive a large distribution of capital gains on which you'd owe taxes very soon. Before you buy, ask the fund when its distributions will be made, and postpone investing if it would adversely influence your tax situation.

Has the portfolio manager changed recently? There are turnovers in mutual fund management fairly often. It's wise to find out whether a fund you are considering has recently changed managers. If it has, you really don't know whether the new manager will match the previous manager's performance record.

proxy A shareholder's written authorization giving someone else the authority to cast his or her vote at a shareholder meeting.

rating An evaluation of a bond issuer's creditworthiness/risk of default by a rating service. Moody's and Standard & Poor's are two well-known rating services.

retirement plan distribution A withdrawal of funds from a retirement plan.

rollover A transfer of assets (which can include cash) from one retirement plan to another. The transfer is tax free. As an IRA holder, you can move assets from your present IRA to another. You can also roll over distributions from a qualified retirement plan into an IRA or to another employer's plan. (See "IRA rollover" for more information.)

round lot The basic unit of trading for a particular security. Most frequently, a round lot is 100 shares.

SARSEP (salary reduction SEP) An employer-sponsored salary reduction plan available to companies with 25 or fewer employees. SARSEPs are similar to 401(k) plans in that they have the same annual contribution limits, but they do not allow for plan loans or hardship withdrawals. As of January 1, 1997, new SARSEP plans may not be opened.

Schwab 1000 Index An index of the 1,000 largest publicly traded U.S. companies as measured by market capitalization (excluding investment companies), representing about 82% of the U.S. stock market's value.

secondary market A market where previously issued securities are traded (usually a stock exchange or the over-the-counter market).

sector/specialty fund A mutual fund that seeks growth by investing in a specific sector of the economy, such as communications, finance, health, natural resources, precious metals, real estate, technology, or utilities.

Securities and Exchange Commission (SEC) The federal government agency, established by Congress, that regulates and protects investors against malpractice in the securities markets.

selling long Selling a security that you own. Also called a "long investment." (See also "selling short.")

selling short Selling a security that you do not own. You borrow the security from your broker and will repurchase or deliver the security to pay back your broker. A cash requirement is needed to secure a short position. Securities involved in margin transactions and/or short transactions are considered "short investments." Selling short has unlimited risk.

SEP-IRA (Simplified Employee Pension plan—IRA) A SEP-IRA is designed for and may be adopted by self-employed individuals, sole proprietors, independent contractors, partnerships, and corporations. One advantage of a SEP-IRA over a Keogh is that it is easier to understand and administer successfully. As with a contributory IRA, you can fund a SEP-IRA each tax year (although annual contributions are not required). Contributions may be made up until the last day of your tax filing deadline, including extensions.

Designed to be an easy-to-manage retirement plan for small companies, the SEP-IRA allows you, the employer, to contribute up to 15% of the compensation of all participating employees. You must contribute the same percentage of income for eligible employees as you contribute for yourself. Contributions paid into an individual employee's SEP-IRA are allowed up to $24,000 or 15% of that individual's compensation, whichever is less. A plan must include all employees who have reached age 21, have worked for the employer during 3 of the 5 preceding years, and have earned a specified amount.

Benefits in a SEP-IRA are always fully vested, and withdrawals must follow the same rules as for an IRA. Like a regular IRA, a SEP-IRA makes an ideal home for potentially high-growth and high-income investments, since earnings compound tax-deferred. Participants in a SEP-IRA or SIMPLE IRA may also still contribute to a regular IRA.

settlement The close of a securities transaction, when you pay your brokerage firm for the securities you've purchased, or when you deliver securities you've sold and receive the proceeds from the sale.

settlement date In a securities transaction, the date when payment is due either to the customer or to the broker, and/or the date when the certificates must be in the broker's possession. For most stock and bond transactions, this is the third business day after the transaction date. For listed options, the settlement date is the day following the trade execution. For mutual funds, it's the same day or the following business day.

share For stocks, a unit of ownership in a company, represented by a stock certificate that specifies the company and the shareholder. For mutual funds, a unit of ownership in the fund.

short-term capital gain A profit on the sale of a stock or mutual fund that the investor owned for less than one year.

SIMPLE 401(k) plan A retirement savings plan, similar to a 401(k) plan, but tailored to the needs of small employers, specifically those with fewer than 100 employees.

SIMPLE IRA plan An employer-sponsored salary reduction retirement plan available only to companies with 100 or less eligible employees. An eligible employee may contribute up to $6,000 of salary each year, and an employer is required to make contributions using one of three contribution "formulas." A SIMPLE IRA is often a very cost-effective retirement plan for the small business.

small capitalization stock The stock of a company that has a market value of under $500 million. Small capitalization (small cap) companies tend to grow more rapidly than larger companies, and they tend to reinvest their profits toward company growth rather than paying dividends. They also tend to be more volatile than larger companies.

small company fund A mutual fund that seeks capital appreciation by investing in stocks or companies with market capitalization of less than $1 billion.

Social Security Money paid out by the U.S. government's social insurance program of the same name, especially during an individual's retirement. Social Security calculates the amount of the monthly benefit that you receive using a formula that's based on the contributions you've made and the age at which you retire. If you're paying Social Security taxes now on average earnings of $45,000 annually, you can expect somewhere around $10,000 annually in Social Security benefits if you retire at the full retirement age. For annual earnings between $18,000 and $45,000, the figure falls between $7,500 and $10,000.

If you retire at the standard age of 65 (which will be increased gradually to 67 by the year 2027), you can receive the full benefit for which you're qualified. But if you retire early, between 62 and the standard age, the amount of your monthly check will be reduced—and the reduction is permanent. You can request a free audit of your account from the Social Security Administration. They'll estimate the amount of monthly benefit you can expect and, more important, give you a chance to correct any errors in your records. Mistakes can be costly, so it's a good idea to ask for an audit periodically to make sure that your Social Security account is correct. Ask for a copy of Form SSA-7004, Request for Earnings & Benefit Estimate Statement. Visit or write the Social Security Administration, or call them 24 hours, toll-free at (800) 772-1213.

split See "stock split."

spousal IRA An IRA established for a nonworking spouse. For the 1997 tax year, a married couple with only one spouse working outside the home may contribute a total of $4,000 to a regular IRA and spousal IRA, as long as the working spouse has earned a minimum of $4,000.

Standard & Poor's 500 (S&P 500) A well-known index comprising New York Stock Exchange (NYSE)–listed companies, as well as a few American Stock Exchange (AMEX)–listed and over-the-counter (or OTC) stocks. The S&P 500 accounts for about 70% of market value of the NYSE. The index is based on the eight-member selection committee's opinion of the country's largest companies, according to market capitalization.

statement An individual's monthly record of his or her trading activity from the brokerage. Your statement is one of the most important documents you'll receive from your brokerage, so take time to understand its sections and explanations.

stock split A technique by which a company's board of directors, after getting the approval of company shareholders, can increase the total number of outstanding shares of its stock. The purpose is often to reduce the price per share of a high-priced stock, making it easier to trade. The outstanding shares of the corporation are simply multiplied. A two-for-one split would, for example, double the number of shares held by each shareholder. There is no increase in capital, and the proportionate ownership of the company's equity remains the same. A split merely decreases share price; it does not change shareholder equity.

stop-limit order An order to buy or sell a security at a specified price or better (the *stop-limit price*), but only after a given stop price has been reached or passed. There is no guarantee of execution.

stop order An order to buy or sell a security once it reaches or trades through a set market price, called the *stop price.* Stop orders automatically become market orders once the set price is reached. Stop prices are not guaranteed. A stop order to buy must be placed at a price higher than the current market price. A stop order to sell must be placed at a price lower than the current market price.

stock A type of security that represents part ownership of a company.

stock certificate A certificate of ownership of one or more specified shares of a company's stock. You cannot buy or sell stock without the certificate, which includes information such as your name or the name of your brokerage firm, the number of shares, the name of the issuer, and the stock's par value.

stock dividend An investor's share of the income earned by a company issuing stock.

STRIPS Zero-coupon Treasury bills issued by the U.S. government at a discount from face value. Interest is paid as a lump sum at maturity. (See also "bond.")

tax deferral The postponement of a tax obligation until sometime in the future.

ticker symbol An abbreviation of a security's name that is used to identify it for trading purposes and in newspaper financial pages and price quotations.

trade date The actual date on which a security is bought or sold. The purchase price is determined by the closing net asset value on this date. The trade date also determines whether you are eligible for dividends.

Treasury bill (T-bill), note, or bond A security issued by the U.S. government.

trust account A legal plan by which a trustor places assets in trust for a beneficiary.

turnover rate The rate, in a percentage, at which a mutual fund annually buys and sells securities. For example, if a fund whose assets totaled $200 million bought and sold $200 million worth of securities in a year, the fund's turnover rate would be 100%.

unit investment trust (UIT) A portfolio of securities that are purchased and held in trust. Units in the trust are then sold to investors, who receive a share of the interest payments and a share of the principal as the bonds in the portfolio mature or are called. Payments are made to investors monthly, quarterly, or semiannually, until all the bonds in the trust mature or are called. Like mutual funds, UITs can be purchased with a relatively small amount of money, and they give you an easy way to diversify your portfolio.

Most UITs are professionally selected portfolios of municipal bonds, but some are devoted to corporate or government bonds, mortgage-backed securities, or even equities. The securities in a

UIT are held to maturity, not continually bought and sold as are the securities in mutual funds. Since UITs are not actively managed, their annual fees are usually lower than those for mutual funds. But they often have higher loads and therefore are often considered longer-term investments. Unlike mutual funds, UITs have a fixed termination date, and most do not allow you to reinvest the earnings.

The value of a UIT moves inversely with market interest rates. If you need to sell your investment before the UIT matures, you may receive more or less than what you paid for it. You can purchase UITs from brokerage firms; the price will include a sales charge. Often the sponsoring brokers for a UIT will also maintain a secondary market for it. Through these brokers, it's often possible to purchase a block of previously traded units. And you can sell your units at their net asset value, receiving your money within three business days.

unrealized capital gain A gain that would be realized if securities were sold.

variable annuity See "annuity."

yield (return) Income received from an investment. Yield is usually represented by a percentage of the investment's share price.

yield to maturity The average annual return on a bond, assuming the bond is held to maturity and all interest payments are reinvested at the same rate. It includes an adjustment for any premium or discount from face value. Comparing yield to maturity is the most common way to compare the value of bonds.

zero-coupon bond A security that does not give periodic interest payments. Instead, you buy the bond at a deep discount from its face value. The interest paid on the bond is the difference between the discounted price and the bond's full face value (which is paid to the investor at maturity). (See also "bond.")

INDEX

ABOUT THE AUTHOR

Charles R. Schwab started investing in 1957, and in 1974 he became a pioneer in the discount brokerage business, guided by the vision of empowering average Americans with information, investment tools, and easy, low-cost access to the stock market. Today, Charles Schwab & Co., Inc., is the nation's largest discount brokerage firm. *Money* magazine recently selected Mr. Schwab as one of the seven people who most influence the economy. He is currently a member of the board of directors of four public companies, a member of the board of trustees for Stanford University, and treasurer of the National Parks Foundation. Mr. Schwab is the founder and chairman of two non-profit organizations, Parents and Educators Resource Center and All Kinds of Minds, both committed to helping students with learning difficulties. The father of five children, he lives with his wife, Helen, in the San Francisco Bay Area.

freemerchant.com
Oh golly.com
e congo.com
Smartage.com
bigstep.com
hoot way.com
bcentral.com
zamora.com
convey.com

NOTES

NOTES

NOTES

NOTES